LISTEN . . . My Children

—and Stay Free

Partners in war and peace

LISTEN . . . My Children

—and Stay Free

Joseph W. Lovoi

VANTAGE PRESS
New York

THIS IS A TRUE STORY. THE NAMES HAVE NOT BEEN CHANGED.

FIRST EDITION

Published by Vantage Press, Inc.
516 West 34th Street, New York, New York 10001

Manufactured in the United States of America
ISBN: 0-533-13225-8

Library of Congress Catalog Card No.: 99-94922

0 9 8 7 6 5 4 3 2 1

THE STORY - "Listen.....My Children"

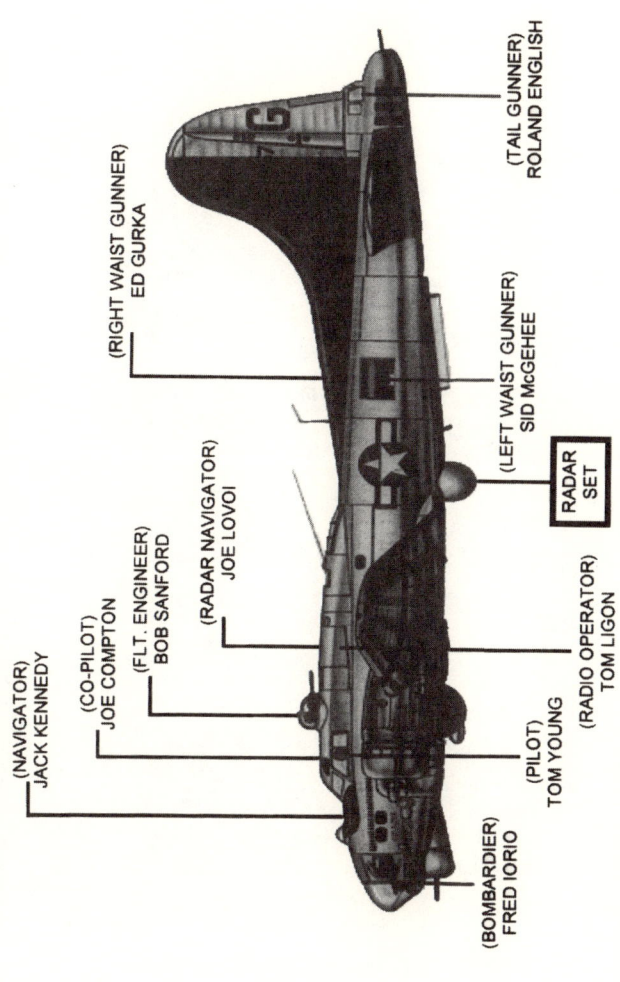

(NAVIGATOR)
JACK KENNEDY

(CO-PILOT)
JOE COMPTON

(FLT. ENGINEER)
BOB SANFORD

(RADAR NAVIGATOR)
JOE LOVOI

(RIGHT WAIST GUNNER)
ED GURKA

(TAIL GUNNER)
ROLAND ENGLISH

(LEFT WAIST GUNNER)
SID McGEHEE

RADAR
SET

(BOMBARDIER)
FRED IORIO

(PILOT)
TOM YOUNG

(RADIO OPERATOR)
TOM LIGON

THE CAST - The Flying Fortress & Crew

The real cost of the American dream

Flying through flak field

Germany:	Italy:	Ireland:	Holland:
Niemann	Lovoi	O'Leary	Van Ace

Typical American Air Force Cadet Backfield—circa 1942

**Lovoi at graduation to Second Lieutenant
Selman Field, Monroe, Louisiana—kneeling, third right**

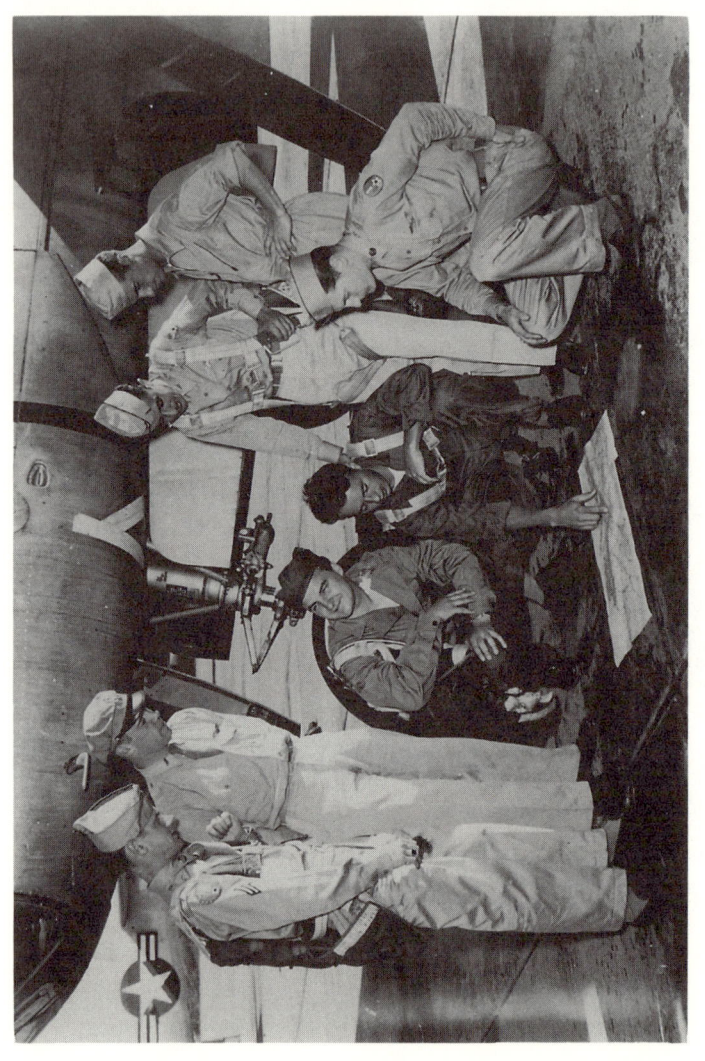

Pre-flight briefing—B-17 training mission, Lovoi—standing fourth right

Contrails over Germany

Bombing through the Undercast

To Posterity

A Challenge

Breed No Generations Who Are Doomed to Repeat This History
A WISH: That This Book Becomes a Spoke in Man's Steering Wheel into His Future

Contents

Acknowledgments

To God—for His mercy

To Christina, my niece—for the courage I needed

To my mother and father, Nancy and Ottavio—for
bearing me

To my siblings and progeny—for their love

To the caterpillar—for spinning the silk that saved me

Author's Note

The true story you are about to read was created by some of the young men and women of the greatest generation of the twentieth century. They were willing to offer the supreme sacrifice, if necessary, in order to preserve the freedoms that our forefathers conceived and died for. These are the freedoms that each generation must preserve for the following generations. Unless we Americans understand and accept this sacred responsibility, the means to realize our own personal American dream will be forfeited.

About the Author

Joseph William Lovoi is a "middle aged" senior citizen and a well-educated pragmatist whose life experiences in the subject of humanities have been contributed to by a number of factors. Because he was a sibling in a large immigrant family, spent his late childhood and early adulthood during the Depression era of the 1930s, and lived in a racially mixed neighborhood, he understands to a large extent what the psychological prime movers of the minority races are. This insight makes it clear to him why living in America is the only hope for minorities to realize their dreams of a better life.

Becoming a soldier in World War II presented him with the opportunity to live with, and examine closely firsthand, not only his reactions under stress, but also his fellow man's reactions to severe life-threatening circumstances. The war experience taught him how to lead, how to follow, and how to obey. The successful conclusion of World War II did rid the world of two ruthless maniacs who were responsible for the sacrifice of millions of human beings. It also provided a platform for the birth of the United Nations Organization, and through the organization of NATO, it also provided the peoples of this planet hope for a lasting peace.

Joseph enlisted in the Army Air Corps when he was twenty-one years old. After thorough and intensive training, he was shipped overseas to the European Theater of

Operations where World War II was doing a pretty good job of blowing up Europe, North Africa, Russia and most of the population that were unfortunate enough to live there. He completed twenty-eight bombing missions over enemy territory as a lead radar navigator as a crew member of the B-17 Flying Fortress. He was shot down on his twenty-ninth mission over Innsbruck, Austria, parachuted into the enemy hands, and shipped to the interrogation center at Wetzlar, Germany.

This true story relates the events of the six months beginning with the takeoff on his last mission, capture, interrogation, solitary confinement, and incarceration in a German prisoner-of-war camp. The story moves quickly to describe a forced march over Silesia during the worst winter in Germany within the last half-century. Survival is described with many pertinent anecdotes that allow the reader to become intimate with the author relating to some of his thoughts, characteristics, and family.

In civilian life he studied hard to become an electrical engineer, followed by a Master's Degree in physics because the study of cosmic rays intrigued his curiosity. He later successfully developed a small business engaged in the manufacture of transportable tactical military systems where he served as CEO for twenty-four years.

His purpose in writing this book is twofold: first to provide the indelible history for his family archives, and second, to articulate a message. The message is to remind posterity that the liberty and freedom they enjoy, and perhaps take for granted, were paid for with the blood and suffering of millions of innocent victims. Stories like this one must be recorded for posterity and serve as reminders, if life as we know it, is to endure on this planet. Each generation must track and remind the succeeding generation about their responsibility to preserve the freedoms and the God-given rights, which were won by our forefathers in the Revolutionary War.

An Intimate Family Portrait

Soon after deciding to write this book, I discovered that besides an interesting story, I needed the patience and relentless incentive to season its chapters in such a manner that the reader's curiosity would never be satisfied. And so, with this aim in mind, I tried to recall the past and choose from its larder those events that would support the unsatisfied curiosity factor. If I have omitted any pertinent data desired by the reader, my apologies will be tempered by the freedom provided in allowing him or her to fill in these omissions by using his or her imagination.

I believe that nearly everyone has felt the urge to write a story at some time or other. I think I can safely say that all people have experienced certain events in their lives that they would like to share. But, in my case, I have compelling reasons to share this part of my life with you, the reader. The reasons are manifold, but in particular, I believe that each generation has the duty to teach its children that freedom is not free, and to remind them just how we secured and nurtured it since the days of our forefathers. The documentation and other evidence of the cost of freedom are available throughout the free world. This true story is one soldier's share of the payment. There are millions more like it, both told and untold. As Winston Churchill once said, "Never in the field of human conflict was so much owed by so many to so few."

Without the preservation of this freedom, there could be no pursuit of happiness, and the realization of the American Dream would not be possible.

This is a true story. The following chapters link together an outline, in candid terms, a series of chronological experiences that I luckily lived through during my hitch in the Army Air Corps in World War II. I was trained to be a Lead Radar Navigator and to fly bombing missions over enemy territory on a B-17 Flying Fortress. This story covers the years between the infamous bombing of Pearl Harbor and the devastating atomic bomb raids on Hiroshima and Nagasaki, two major industrialized Japanese cities. My hope is that this story, in some positive way, will continue to remind us and those yet to come, that human tragedies that claimed over 32,000,000 military lives, and the use of atomic power to obliterate millions more, must never happen again.

And now I am going to switch to the third person style of writing in order to present this story with maximum dramatic effect.

The main character you will meet is a twenty-two-year-old young man by the name of Joseph William Lovoi. He was the sixth issue of a brood numbering eight siblings. Add along with this brood a mother and a father, Nancy and Ottavio, and that made up the Lovoi family. All eight children were born at home, not an uncommon practice for those days. Ottavio was a tailor, perhaps one of the best of his day. He was born in Italy and served in the Italian army throughout World War I. He was married to Nancy, who was also born in Italy. They were both eighteen years old at that time. They realized that if they were to find happiness and opportunity anywhere, it would be in America, the land of opportunity. So sometime around 1906, they came to America, settled in Gloversville, New York, and had their first child, Anna. She was also called Annina.

But soon, homesickness overcame Nancy and sometime around 1911, Ottavio took his family back to Italy for a visit. During that prolonged stay WWI broke out, and all emigration by draft-age males was prohibited by the Italian government. Ottavio was conscripted into the Italian Army and was fortunate to live through the war with only a minor wound. But it was not until 1920 that the Lovoi family could return to America. By that time Anna had been joined by Rosa, called Rosalie, and Benedict, called Ben, and Emanuel, called Sam, and Anne, called Nerina.

Ottavio returned to America several months before Nancy and the five children in order to establish a domicile. When Nancy and the five children did arrive in America, Ottavio settled them down in Gloversville, New York, where he found work.

Joseph was born in Gloversville, New York, on July 30, 1921. He was delivered at home by an Irish country doctor, whose first name was Joseph. Herein is found a vignette. After the birth, the doctor began to file the birth data for the town records. He asked Ottavio what name he should enter on the birth certificate for his new son. Ottavio told the doctor that the child's name was Giuseppe. The doctor casually filled in the name as Joseph, the Anglicized version of Giuseppe. Of course, Joseph never did have the opportunity to thank the sly doctor personally, but he did mentally thank him on many occasions since that time.

The family religion was strict Roman Catholic: baptism, confirmation, Mass every Sunday and holy days,

Holy Communion, and of course, Christian names for the children. They were all named after relatives. The practice of naming the children after their relatives was a common one for children sired by immigrant parents. It was meant to show respect for the members of the family tree. Since most of the living relatives remained in the native land, this practice was an attempt to tie the family tree occupants together in both worlds, the old and the new.

Many of the immigrating newcomers to America tended to settle as ethnic groups, and in ethnic locations. For example, the North End, a part of Boston, Massachusetts, was settled by nearly 100 percent Italian immigrants. When Joseph was about five years old, he and his family moved from Gloversville, New York, to Cambridge, Massachusetts. His next fifteen years were spent living on Jay Street and then Hancock Street, both locales being within the overlapping shadows of Harvard College and the Massachusetts Institute of Technology (MIT).

Most of the residences in these two locales were multi-family units. The inhabitants were nearly all a mixture of people who had emigrated from England, Germany, France, Italy, Poland, Ireland, Lithuania, Africa, and Southeast Asia. The children were mostly first-generation Americans. It was a credit to the parents of these families to see how well they all got along with each other. They were hard-working, no nonsense, law-abiding neighbors, eager to become American citizens and weave the strong social fabric from the values America was founded for: freedom, liberty, and opportunity. They were thirsty for an education and its promise for economic blessings.

Regardless of individual backgrounds, when one family within the neighborhood needed help in any way, the community was there, prepared to assist in every way possible. They spoke with one voice when it came to patriotism and loyalty. You would think that the United States was their birth country. They studied hard to become good American citizens. Their staunch loyalty, to their adopted country, poured the mold for the cornerstones and foundations of the future generations that made America great.

Joseph's early life had been relatively uneventful. He hawked newspapers as a kid, worked in a grocery store as a young adult, and studied electrical engineering at night at MIT after he graduated from high school. He grew up during the Great Depression of the 1930's. Shortly after Pearl Harbor, he enlisted in the Army Air Corps, and thus he began his journey into manhood.

Prologue

It was cold. No, it was bone-chilling cold that winter of 1944–1945 in Sagan, Germany, where Stalag Luft III was located. Sagan is a small German town just outside the border of Poland about ninety miles east by southeast of Berlin. Stalag Luft III was a large prisoner-of-war compound that housed thousands of Allied flying officers who were captured as they parachuted from their crippled aircrafts into enemy hands.

And now it was just a few days before Christmas 1944 and First Lieutenant Joseph Lovoi was lying in his slat-bottom wooden bunk in one of the many barracks located in the North Camp of the Stalag. It was a quiet late evening. He shook his head slowly as he reviewed the series of events that had culminated in his capture and captivity. He closed his eyes, and for the hundredth time, he tried to blot out any visible clues that confirmed his predicament to be real and permanent. His body shivered as it begged for that elusive tranquilizer, sleep. But, his young, wide-awake mind insisted on returning his memory to the tragic scenes of his last bombing mission over enemy territory. In fact, it had been his twenty-ninth mission and he was doing his usual thing, leading a group of sixty-four bombers to a target in Austria, the marshaling yards at Innsbruck. From the time that the wheels of his B-17 Flying Fortress broke the gravitational hold of the runway at Foggia, Italy, he had no clue that he was on a one-way mission, his longest mission. He had flown through this scenario so often that he never dreamed that this would be the last time that he would lead his bomb group over an enemy target.

Although he had crossed and criss-crossed the imposing range of mountains just north of the Italian border many times, he still marveled at the snow-blanketed Austrian Alps as they rose into the cold atmosphere that hugged them. He still could feel the thrilling excitement as the pilot, Tom Young, steered the bomb group over a small town just south of Innsbruck, called Mayrhofen. This town was the Initial Point (IP) of the bomb run which would terminate over the Innsbruck marshaling yards. The approaches to the initial point were completely socked in with a thick undercast necessitating Lovoi's use of his airborne radar to locate the Initial Point, (IP), and to lead the trailing bombers over the bomb run to Innsbruck. Only the highest peaks of the Alps could be seen at this altitude, as they stabbed through the cloud cover.

The leg from the northern coast of the Adriatic Sea to Mayrhofen was successfully accomplished and the sixty-four bombers were in a tight formation as they encountered the enemy anti-aircraft flak on their bomb run. Halfway through the bomb run, ABLE ONE, the lead bomber, triggered open its bomb bay doors. Instantly, the other sixty-three B-17s followed suit and triggered open their bomb bay doors. Now there were 640, five-hundred-pound bombs poised and ready to do their damage as soon as ABLE ONE signalled by dropping its load. The enemy anti-aircraft gunners fired barrage after barrage at the oncoming airborne armada. Much of the bursting shells (flak) found targets within the wings and bellies of the flying bombers at thirty-thousand feet over the target.

The target was still invisible to the naked eye, but the exploding flak filled the bomb run alley through which the bombers had to fly. Several aircraft were hit and began to lose altitude. ABLE ONE's bombardier, Captain Iorio, finally was able to locate the target through a break in the clouds, and took over the responsibility from Lovoi for the bomb run. At the precise moment the bombs were released from the leader's bomb bay, followed by six-hundred-thirty additional bombs from the rest of the bomb group. Lovoi heard Iorio scream "Bombs Away!"

And then it happened. ABLE ONE caught a direct hit from the anti-aircraft fire that raked its fuselage from the forward chin turret in the nose to the radio and radar compartment just behind the flight deck. The B-17 was catapulted to an almost vertical nose-up position scattering maps, parachutes, ammunition, and other loose flight gear throughout. Lovoi grabbed the handles of his radar set and hung on. The bomber swung through its vertical nose-up position down to a near vertical dive as its #3 engine burst into flames, sending a long trail of orange-and-black flame from its nacelle.

The #4 engine was also malfunctioning. Its propeller was spinning uncontrollably, making it more difficult for the pilots to bring the bomber under some control. Lovoi looked past his radar set to the radio man, Tom Ligon, and saw him grimace as he grabbed his right thigh in pain. Blood was spurting through his gloved fingers from a gaping wound. He had been hit. The bomb bay doors were still open. One of the ten bombs was hung up in the bomb bay and was dangling dangerously from one anchor. As the pilots fought desperately to extinguish the fire on #3 engine, and feather #4, (stop the propeller from spinning), the rest of the crew were pinned to their seats and positions by the centrifugal force, as the crippled

3

bomber nosed into a steep dive. The co-pilot, Major Compton, activated the "Bail Out" button to signal the dreaded command. The ominous sound of its wail stunned the entire crew as they plunged earthward in their fiery casket.

Lovoi nervously turned on his side as he lay twitching in his bunk. The cold darkness was adumbrated by eerie silence. Each time he relived these memories, they succeeded in eroding a little more of the neatly patterned black-and-white fabric of his world. He even began to doubt the possible existence of the American Dream. Idealism began to give way to realism. His sense of immortality was shaken but not forsaken. Maybe he was immortal.

How else could he and millions of other young soldiers around the world be willing to put up their very lives to preserve the freedoms for themselves and their posterity, while hoping to survive the ravages of that greedy god, War? He finally fell asleep.

I

The Last Takeoff

The morning of November 16, 1944, arrived cold and dry. It was a still morning. The winds were calm and the birds had yet to awaken. You would have a hard time to suspect that a heavy bomber air base, part of the Fifteenth U.S. Air Force, was located here, just about seventy-five miles east of Rome, Italy. In fact the air base was on the outskirts of Foggia, a center where farmers lived but commuted to their farms on the surrounding flat land. Part of this flat land was restructured into a temporary heavy bomber base.

It was at this base that Lieutenant Joseph Lovoi served his military tour of duty as a Lead Radar Navigator. He was assigned to the 774th Bomb Squadron, one of the four squadrons that made up the 463rd Bomb Group. Each squadron consisted of sixteen B-17 Flying Fortress bombers, and hence the group totaled sixty-four bombers. Each bomber carried 10 airmen, totalling 640 in the 463rd Bomb Group. Each bomber cradled ten 500-pound bombs, making a total of 640 bombs for delivery to the Nazi targets throughout Germany, Poland, Italy, Yugoslavia, and Czechoslovakia. Each mission then carried 640 airmen and 640 bombs.

When the bombers reached their targets, there was no guarantee that the weather would cooperate and give the bombardier a cloudless view of them. So, the lead aircraft of each squadron was equipped with an airborne search radar that could "see" through any undercast and make the targets visible to the radar navigator. The radar search antenna of the lead bomber was located in the ball turret, so each squadron lead B-17 included a lead radar navigator in the place of the ball turret gunner.

The airborne radar system radiated electronic energy that easily penetrated the undercast, "painted" the target, and reflected its exact location to the radar navigator. He then would enter this data into the bomb sight for processing and to allow the bomb sight to accurately release its deadly load and destroy the target. If, however, the weather over the target was clear, the bombardier fed the target location data into the bomb sight and the radar navigator just went along for the ride. Upon release of the bomb load by the lead aircraft, the remaining B-17's in the formation released their bomb loads at almost the exact same instant. At this point, the vertical separation of the B-17's in the formation was critical to avoid dropping bombs on errant Flying Fortresses. The enemy targets included air fields, oil refineries, munition factories, aircraft assembly plants, ball bearing factories, bridges, troop concentrations, railroad marshaling yards, and industrial complexes.

And so the stillness of this cold November morning at the Foggia air base was interrupted by half a dozen duty sergeants as they swiftly scurried from tent to tent rousing those airmen who were scheduled to fly. It was 3:00 A.M. when one of the sergeants flashlighted his way into Lieutenant Lovoi's tent and gently shook him awake. "It's three o'clock, sir," he whispered. Lovoi lifted himself up on one elbow and replied, "Thanks, Sergeant."

A moment later the messenger was gone. Lovoi shivered a little as thoughts of this mission took shape in his mind. He was a veteran of twenty-eight missions. His position in those missions alternated from squadron lead to wing man. But this mission, his twenty-ninth, would be his first mission as Group Radar Navigator Lead. His bomber would be the first of sixty-four B-17's to fly down the bomb run. He wondered which target had been selected by Operations Command for that day. He quietly finished putting on his flying clothes and slipped out of the tent, being careful not to awaken those occupants who were not scheduled to fly. The chilly presence of the pre-dawn atmosphere made him shiver a little more. The early darkness made it difficult to see the heavily trodden trail that led to the mess hall. He really was not hungry, but he knew from experience that by the time mid-morning came around, he would be.

The lieutenant pushed his way through the mess hall tent flap and headed for the food counter. He picked up two eggs, over easy, a glass of reconstituted frozen orange juice, and a cup of hot black coffee. He sat by himself as he swallowed the meal, hardly realizing what he was eating. He wanted to think. He wanted to screw up his courage. He wanted to mentally review his role as the lead navigator. He might even have wished for a clear target, but he wasn't sure. It was a lot of responsibility for a twenty-two-year-old soldier, but he remembered that when he had finished his training in the States, his flight instructor commented on his rating sheet that he was a potential Group or Wing Navigator. The lieutenant was determined to realize his instructor's faith in his ability.

He quickly gathered his flight bag and left the mess hall. On the way to the briefing tent he passed some of his ground crew buddies. They spoke words of good luck as he passed them, and without breaking stride, he wheeled and gave them the "thumbs up" gesture as his acknowledgment of their concern. The briefing tent was about fifty yards beyond the mess hall.

As Lieutenant Lovoi drew closer to the briefing tent, he could hear the muffled voices of those airmen inside as they grew louder and clearer. It seemed to him that there was an unwarranted excitement in the air. Maybe he was a little nervous. He did feel more comfortable as he greeted some of his flying comrades and engaged them in casual conversation. Suddenly, he was not cold any more. Actually, he could feel some dampness under the collar of his sheepskin flying jacket. He loosened the collar as he edged his way toward the dais at the end of the tent.

The large vertical mission map stood on the dais like a silent honor guard. The map was covered with a blanket. Not until the audience was complete and not until the security guards were posted outside of the tent would it reveal its target identification. It would not do if the enemy learned the identification of the target even before the B-17's were airborne. It would give the enemy ample time to prepare a devastating reception.

Only pilots, co-pilots, bombardiers, and navigators were allowed to attend the briefing session. The noncommissioned officers were busy helping the ground crews load and fuel the bombers on the flight line. They were also busy pre-flighting their flight positions to be sure that machine guns, oxygen systems, heating circuits, flak suits, parachutes, and food rations were either operating properly or present.

The briefing officer, a major in rank, rapped his map pointer on the top of the map frame. His call for attention was quickly heeded as the room became engulfed in silence. The major hesitated for but a moment. Then, "Gentlemen," he began, "the target for today is Munich, Germany." The immediate reaction from the airmen was continued silence. But only for a moment. The reaction quickly changed to murmuring and babbling as comments were exchanged among the airmen concerning the bloody cost of visiting Munich in the past. Munich was the second most heavily defended target in Germany, Berlin being the first.

As the din spilled over the gathering, the briefing officer slowly walked over to the covered map and removed the blanket. There was the regional map of Italy, Austria, and southern Germany. A broad red crayon line ran from the Air Force base in Foggia, due east about a hundred miles to a central point in the Adriatic Sea. It continued northwesterly to the northern coast of Italy, due north across the Udine Valley in northern Italy, made a zigzag maneuver over the Austrian Alps, due west to the small town of Starnberg, the IP, located just fifteen miles west by southwest of the target, the industrial complex in Munich, Germany.

The major proceeded to elucidate regarding the high priority of the target and just how effective the production from the industrial complex was in supporting the enemy forces. This target was to be destroyed at all costs. The briefing officer then wished the airmen "good luck" and left the podium. The airmen then gathered in three groups: pilots with Operations to discuss tactics and flight procedures; bombardiers with Armament to discuss the bombing sequences and bomb sight calibration; and navigators with Weather and Intelligence to discuss the location of enemy anti-aircraft flak batteries, weather conditions en route both ways, conditions over the target area, and contingency procedures in the event of aircraft damage due to enemy actions.

The town of Starnberg was chosen as the IP because it presented a clear bomb run to the target with the prevailing winds from the west to aid the bomb group's speed and minimize any drift effects as the bombs dropped from the thirty-thousand-foot release altitude. The IP is that point in the sky where the whole group of sixty-four bombers align themselves in tight formation and are pointed in the direction of the target. The distance between the IP and the target is the bomb run. It is during this time on the bomb run that the lead bombardier corrects his bomb sight settings for temperature, pressure, and any drift.

When the lead bomber's bomb bay doors are triggered open, the rest of the bombardiers in the group trigger their bomb bay doors open. When the lead bomber drops its bombs, the rest of the bombers drop their bombs. The opening of the bomb bay doors is done by the bombardiers who fly in the very nose of the B-17's and have a bird's-eye view of the lead aircraft in front of them. The weather briefing predicted clear skies en route all the way to the Alps, but the weather over the target area was "iffy." This meant that the bomb run had a fifty-fifty chance of being accomplished visually by the bombardier, Captain Iorio, otherwise electronically by Lieutenant Lovoi using his radar set to "see" the target if there was an undercast.

When the respective briefings were over, Lovoi hopped aboard a flight line truck with his other comrades and reviewed the mission briefing in his mind. He was determined, if called upon, to find the IP and lead the group over the most accurate bomb run he had ever led.

His philosophy was simple; either destroy the target today, or come back and do it tomorrow or the next day, until it was destroyed. The flak over this target was acknowledged to be heavy, accurate, and devastating. The Luftwaffe, the German Airforce, was predicted to be active in this region. But there was no way around it. This target had to be destroyed.

The squealing of the flight line truck's brakes broke his reverie. Lovoi jumped off the truck and made his way to the first bomber on the flight line. This aircraft was designated ABLE ONE for positional identification purposes. It was at the top of the diamond-shaped, four aircraft element that would lead the group. Each diamond element consisted of four B-17's. Four such aircraft elements made up the 774th Bomb Squadron. The other three members of the lead element were designated ABLE TWO, ABLE THREE, and ABLE FOUR. The second element of the 774th Bomb Squadron, the BAKER element, consisting of BAKER ONE, BAKER TWO, BAKER THREE, BAKER FOUR, and they flew just to the right, behind and slightly above the ABLE element.

Likewise, The CHARLIE diamond-shaped element consisted of CHARLIE ONE, CHARLIE TWO, CHARLIE THREE, and CHARLIE FOUR. Its flying position was also behind the ABLE element, but slightly below and to the left of it. Finally the DOG element brought up the rear of the 774th Bomb Squadron. It flew below and well back of the ABLE element and just behind the BAKER and CHARLIE elements. The most difficult positions to fly were in the DOG element. Except for time on the bomb run, the DOG pilots spent the entire mission time, seven to ten hours depending on the range of the target, looking up at the ABLE Lead elements jockeying their positions in order to maintain their places in the formation.

A-1	ABLE ONE	B-1	BAKER ONE
A-2	ABLE TWO	B-2	BAKER TWO
A-3	ABLE THREE	B-3	BAKER THREE
A-4	ABLE FOUR	B-4	BAKER FOUR

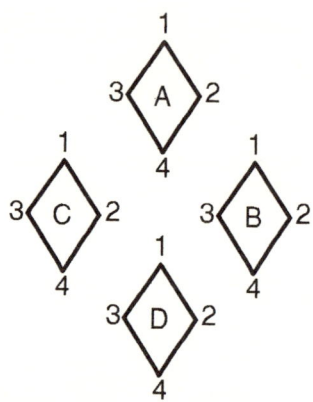

C-1	CHARLIE ONE	D-1	DOG ONE
C-2	CHARLIE TWO	D-2	DOG TWO
C-3	CHARLIE THREE	D-3	DOG THREE
C-4	CHARLIE FOUR	D-4	DOG FOUR

This is a plan view of one of the four squadrons that make up the 463 Bomb Group. It consists of sixteen Bombers flying the diamond formation. The Baker elements fly above the Able elements. The Charlie elements fly below the Able elements, and the Dog elements fly lowest of all, directly below the Able elements, but behind the Baker and Charlie elements.

This is a plan view of he 463rd Bomb Group.
It is made up of four squadrons consisting of
sixteen bombers each or sixty-four total.

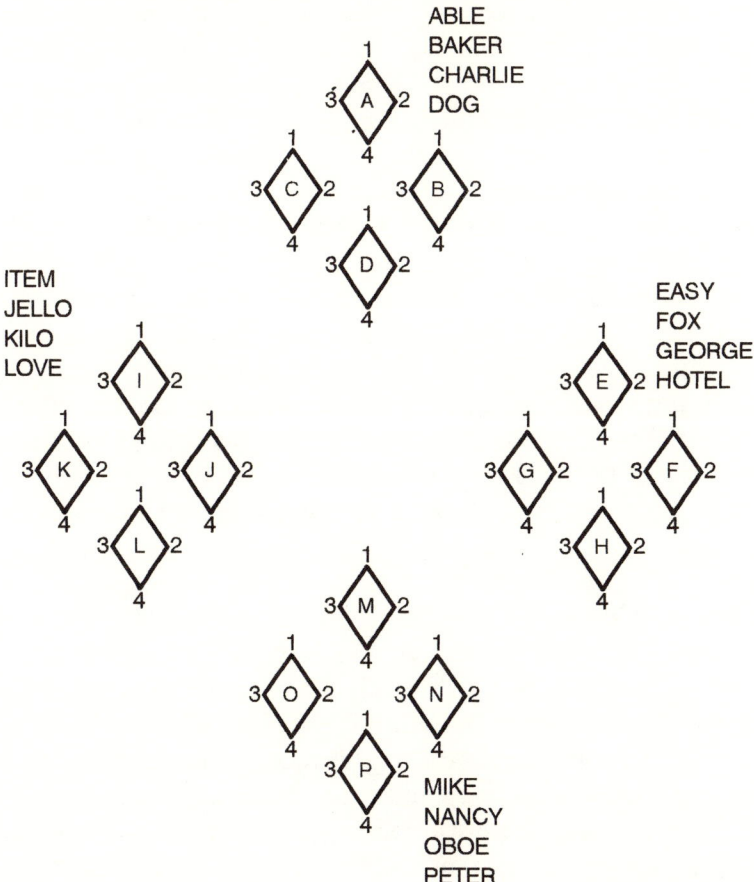

The scene around ABLE ONE, nicknamed by its crew "Wichita Belle," was a busy one. The ground crew was loading fuel in the bomber's wing tanks, placing oxygen tanks, flak suits, bombs, food rations, and machine gun cartridges into the bomber's belly. The flying crew members were pre-flighting their respective positions for proper and safe operation. Lieutenant Lovoi looked down the endless flight line and marveled at the long line of graceful aerodynamic B-17 Flying Fortresses poised at the "ready," waiting for their pilots to push the buttons on the cockpit's control panel, which would squirt life into their multi-engined power plants, so they could race into the skies and complete their appointed rounds.

He delayed boarding the Wichita Belle because he was expecting the base chaplain to show up, as he faithfully did before all bombing missions. It was now nearly 5:30 A.M. The dawn was lifting on the eastern horizon, allowing streaks of light to slip through the stratus cloud layers. The chaplain's jeep did arrive, bringing the chaplain right up to the bomber and under its wing. Those crew members who desired to receive Holy Communion gathered before the chaplain. Some of them stood and some of them knelt. Lieutenant Lovoi dropped to one knee and received the hard white wafer into his dry mouth. He found it hard to swallow. It was not until he entered Wichita Belle through the escape hatch, that he finished swallowing the Holy Eucharist.

He tossed his flight bag through the opening and then pulled himself up into the fuselage where he retrieved the bag. It contained such vital gear as goggles, oxygen mask, navigation tools, gloves for his heating system, and his good luck charm, a small plastic white elephant. It was after six o'clock before the ground crew

finished their tasks of loading and checking routines. The air crew were all in place and ready to roll.

Lieutenant Tom Young, the pilot, pulled back his cockpit window and yelled down to the flight director, "Ready to start engines." The director, who was on the tarmac and within sight of the pilot, nodded his head and stood by. Then Tom yelled down, "Clear left." This command was to warn the ground personnel that he was about to start engine #1. After assuring himself that there were no personnel under the wing, the flight director yelled back at Lieutenant Young, "Clear left." Lieutenant Young then goosed the throttle several times, primed engine #1, and hit the start button.

Like a lazy sleeping tiger who was suddenly awakened, the engine roared its challenge. At first it belched black smoke and orange flame through its nacelle, and slowly cleaned up its act so only orange-white flames were exhausting from its tail pipe. It was an eerie sight, this hot flame when framed against the now pale gray sky. The noise rose to a crescendo as Tom Young tested the engine to nearly its maximum RPM's. The same start-up procedure was carried out for engines number 2, 3, and 4. The deafening noise shattered the early morning silence and must have been heard all the way to Rome.

Each of the four engines were tested to nearly their maximum RPM's. All the while, the wheel brakes were locked to keep the bomber from lurching forward. Each engine was tested separately. When the flight crew was satisfied that the B-17 was airworthy, they throttled the engines to idle and called the control tower. Major Joe Compton, the co-pilot, pressed his transmit button and said, "ABLE ONE ready to taxi." The tower responded, "ABLE ONE cleared to taxi and hold, off the end of the active runway."

Now Pilot Tom Young, Co-pilot Joe Compton, Bombardier Captain Iorio, Navigator Lieutenant John Kennedy, and all the gunners waved to the ground crew as the huge, heavily laden bomber lumbered its way slowly to a spot off the end of the runway where it would warm up under full power. During this warm-up, each engine had to exhibit the proper temperature and pressure readings in order to permit takeoff. This same routine was concurrently being followed by the other sixty-three aircraft sequentially down the line. The total time allowed to pre-flight and getting the whole bomb group off the runway and into the air was in the vicinity of ninety minutes.

ABLE ONE was now ready. Joe Compton called the tower and announced, "ABLE ONE ready for takeoff." The tower responded, "ABLE ONE cleared to the end of the runway, and hold."

At this command, Tom Young urged his B-17 to the end of the runway, swung it around so it was facing the long narrow, steel matted corridor, applied pressure to the brakes, and gave a final visual check across the cockpit instruments. He knew all too well that once the bomber was on its roll there was no turning back. The heavy aircraft rocked back and forth like a track runner waiting for the starter's gun. The waiting moments seemed long. And then the wait was finally over.

A crisp command came over the radio to the pilot, "ABLE ONE, you are cleared for takeoff." Ever so slowly the Wichita Belle began its roll down the runway. Both pilots applied full throttle and full rich fuel mixture to the controls. The bomber seemed eager to respond. Its speed was increasing exponentially as it sought that margin that would allow its wings to create the needed lift to somehow raise the plane, full bomb load, full fuel load, ten airmen, and ten heavy flak suits high enough to clear the row of trees at the end of the runway and rise into the sky.

As the B-17 passed the halfway mark on the runway, the order to clear ABLE TWO for takeoff was heard over the radio. And just as ABLE ONE was about to clear the trees at the end of the runway, the order to clear ABLE THREE for takeoff could be heard as well. The traffic on the runway was controlled so that there were three B-17's on it at all times during the takeoff phase of the mission; one just lifting, one in the middle picking up takeoff speed, and one at the starting end as it began its roll.

ABLE ONE barely cleared the trees just beyond the end of the runway. The crew members breathed a collective sigh of relief. The mission time clock had started, and ABLE ONE's fate was sealed. It flew straight ahead, carving a wide circle over the base, picking up its wingmen ABLE TWO, ABLE THREE, and ABLE FOUR as it gently increased its altitude. Unless the lead aircraft flew at a precise speed and climbed at a steady angle, its wingmen would have a difficult time creating the diamond formation without wasting precious fuel to catch up. Lovoi sat back on his seat, closed his eyes, and whispered an Act of Contrition. It was his custom to pray this prayer during every takeoff and every landing.

II
The Longest Mission

During the slow, wide helical spiral from ground zero to ten thousand feet, Tom Young was concentrating on his air speed, climb angle, and forward visibility. Major Joe Compton, the co-pilot, was busy adjusting the throttles and mixture controls to keep the engines synchronized as the altitude and pressure changes affected their performance. The flight engineer was reporting to the pilot the presence and location of the ABLE element wingmen. The plan was for the entire bomb group of four squadrons to be in a loose diamond formation by the time ABLE leader reached the mission starting point over Foggia. This was the point on the mission map that began with a broad red crayon mark and headed due east.

A tight formation was not necessary on this phase of the mission. A loose formation gave the pilots some room for relative ease and relaxation. The tight formation was mandatory during those legs of the mission in which the bomb group was over enemy territory, and especially on the bomb run. The tighter the formation, the smaller the target for anti-aircraft gunners and Luftwaffe fighter activity. And at the same time, the tighter the formation, the more concentrated the bomb drop over the target, and the more effective the gunners' combined protective fire at the German fighter aircraft that attacked the formation.

And so it was on that November morning, at approximately seven o'clock that Lieutenant Kennedy gave Lieutenant Young an easterly heading propelling ABLE ONE and the 463rd Bomb Group on the first leg of the mission. Captain Iorio reminded the crew members that it was time to put on their oxygen masks and that he would take an oxygen check from each position at every thousand feet of altitude throughout the mission. Lovoi turned on his radar set and began to scan that part of the planet that lay between the Italian and Yugoslavian coastlines, historically known as the Adriatic Sea.

The B-17's were unpressurized and unheated. The four power plants droned insistently in the airmen's ears. But after several hours into the mission, the drone became a part of the background nuisance experienced by most airmen. Lovoi was very aware of the responsibility he bore. The mission's success or failure could be laid right on his back. He was determined to carry out his job well. This meant that he must be absolutely sure of his position for every mile of the journey. The weather changes over southern Europe were known to be swift and unpredictable.

There were sixty-four planes carrying 640 airmen who were flying just feet apart from each other in a relatively loose formation. Although it was Lieutenant Kennedy's responsibility to navigate the group along the mission, Lieutenant Lovoi used his navigational expertise to confirm Kennedy's "fixes." But if the weather suddenly "socked in," then the roles were reversed and Lieutenant Lovoi would direct the pilot's headings and Lieutenant Kennedy would back him up as best he could, using "dead reckoning" calculations. Of course, the enemy did not provide any navigational aids to the Allies.

On the contrary, they consistently electronically jammed the radio and radar receivers of the bomber groups as the Allies carried out their daily bombing raids. And in a reciprocal action, the bomber group waist gunners would periodically toss out of their waist positions a material known as "chaf." It had the property of reflecting false location data to the enemy ground-search radar systems, causing them to fire their anti-aircraft shells harmlessly off target.

And so Lieutenant Lovoi began to mark his radar maps studiously with the group's exact location at every reasonable checkpoint. The mission was uneventful on the leg from Foggia to the Adriatic, and from the Adriatic north over the enemy coastline into the Udine Valley of Italy. Even the weather was cooperating. The late morning broke into a clear sunny day and Lovoi's spirit was raised with optimism. But it was not to be. Major Compton alerted the crew that ABLE ONE was about to cross into enemy territory and that every man would be needed to watch the skies for "bandits," the Luftwaffe. Captain Iorio was in the middle of the fifteen-thousand-foot oxygen check. Lovoi verified Kennedy's fix over the Italian coast. The loose formation was instructed to tighten up.

Lovoi began to pick up reflections of the Italian Alps on his radar set. The bomber group was right on course and right on schedule. ABLE ONE was just breaking eighteen-thousand feet when Lovoi noticed that Sergeant Ligon, the radio operator, had adjusted his headset and was listening intently to something coming in on his radio set. Ligon grabbed his note pad and pencil and began writing furiously. His face, what could be seen of it behind his oxygen mask, showed concern. He glanced over at Lovoi and shrugged his shoulders.

When he had finished taking the radio message, he addressed Major Compton on the intercommunication system. He reported that he had just received a radio message from home base in Foggia instructing the 463rd Bomb Group to abort the mission and return to base. The major uttered an oath and reluctantly gave the order to turn the group around and head back to base. Turning a formation of sixty-four bombers to a 180° heading is no easy task without scattering some wing men. But Tom Young was one of the more experienced pilots in the group as he slowly began the maneuver without losing or gaining any altitude.

When the airborne armada was about halfway turned, Joe Compton, the co-pilot, called the radio operator on the intercom and directed him to verify the abort message. Ligon got on the secure transmit channel immediately and tried to raise the radio station on the base in Foggia. It took several minutes to succeed in raising the base. When Ligon asked for confirmation of the abort message, the base commander was furious. He disclaimed any knowledge of such a transmission and insisted that the mission be carried out as planned. And now it was Major Compton's turn to be on the hot seat. The return-to-base maneuver had used up precious fuel, which made it impossible for the Group to reach the primary target, Munich, and still have enough fuel left to return to Foggia.

Major Compton and Captain Iorio got together on the intercom to discuss which alternate target should be selected. Tom Young, in the meantime, was turning the Group back on its original course until further advised as to the location of the alternate target. Iorio recommended that the marshaling yards at Innsbruck, Austria, were high on the priority list. He also reasoned that Innsbruck was close to Switzerland and in the event of the need for a neutral country for disabled B-17's and/or parachuting airmen, Switzerland made sense. Compton agreed with Iorio and asked Kennedy for a choice of a new IP for the bomb run to Innsbruck, and a heading to it. But now the weather was closing in.

The Bomb Group was climbing through twenty-thousand feet and a solid undercast was forming below it. Lovoi and his radar were pressed into service and directed to give the pilot his selection of an IP and a heading to it. Since the Group had no visual contact with the ground, Lovoi picked up the Group's position on his radar, chose the small town of Mayrhofen just fifteen miles east by southeast of Innsbruck as the new IP, measured a heading to the IP on his map, and gave it to Lieutenant Young. Slowly Young swung ABLE ONE onto that heading and the rest of the Bomb Group followed like a flock of geese. Lovoi switched to the sector scan mode of his radar. This mode updated the data on the screen at a faster rate than the orbital scan mode. Lovoi picked his way across the Alps, identifying every checkpoint he recognized on the way. He calculated his time to Mayrhofen.

The flying time from his position over the Italian Alps to Mayrhofen was approximately twenty-five minutes. His eyes stayed glued to the radar screen. No one said a word. Only Iorio's oxygen checks broke the ominous silence. The risk of navigating over a mountain range by radar is that all radar returns begin to look alike on the screen. So it is extremely important to positively identify your position and not get lost. Once lost, it is very difficult to relocate your position.

Just as the ETA (estimated time of arrival) to Mayrhofen had elapsed, Lovoi miraculously spotted the little town. He realized his voice trembled with excitement, but the news that ABLE ONE was over the IP was exciting to the pilots and the rest of the crew. Young carefully aligned his B-17, the Wichita Belle, and the rest of the Bomb Group on the bomb run heading to the marshaling yards at Innsbruck. Captain Iorio turned his bomb sight settings to the proper altitude, air speed, and heading. Lovoi and Iorio were now in private communication. Lovoi picked up the target easily on his radar set and gave Iorio its coordinates. As if to verify the accuracy of the formation's position, a black column of exploding flak could be seen piercing the undercast directly over the intended target. This was the reception the Germans had prepared.

At the beginning of the bomb run, several adjustments had to be made to the bomb sight to correct for drift. Iorio hit the bomb bay door control button. ABLE ONE's bomb bay doors were open. And in sequence the bomb bay doors of the rest of the squadron and the rest of the group were opened. Lovoi fed another correction to Iorio so the bomb sight would remain on target. As if the temperature was not cold enough, 60° below zero Centigrade, the cold blast of frigid air gushing through the open bomb bay reminded the crew members that it was truly winter. Five miles from Innsbruck, Lovoi asked Captain Iorio, "Fred, can you see the target?" And Fred replied, "Hell no, I can't see any breaks in the clouds yet."

Lovoi glanced at his radar screen and verified that the ABLE ONE was still on target. The bomb sight was processing the data that he had fed its computer through Iorio. So far it appeared that the bombs would be released at the optimum moment assuring a direct hit. The moment of release was just seconds away when Iorio broke the intercom silence. "I see it! I can see it!" he screamed. During the time left for the bomb release, Iorio adjusted the bomb sight cross hairs squarely on the target and watched as they held their position. The anti-aircraft flak was getting heavier.

Contrails over Germany

Lovoi could actually hear some of the shrapnel impact on the aluminum structure of his B-17. The flak continued to grow in intensity as the bomb group advanced toward the target. Flying down the bomb run was like entering a black tunnel. The black explosions were accurate and effective. But the bomb group had to stay its course if it was to deliver the bombs on the target. The flak explosions at thirty-thousand feet caused ABLE ONE to bump a little on its flight path, and then it happened. Iorio was heard to yell *"BOMBS AWAY!"* This announcement was immediately followed by a loud explosion in the forward area of ABLE ONE. And then it felt like some giant force had lifted the Witchita Belle into a stall position only to drop it back down in a steep dive toward the sharp icy peaks of the Austrian Alps. ABLE ONE was mortally wounded! The centrifugal force created by this unexpected maneuver pinned Lovoi in his seat. He thought he heard a cry. He turned his head toward Ligon, the radio operator.

Ligon was writhing in pain as he grabbed his right thigh. Blood was oozing from his thigh through his gloved fingers and almost freezing on the spot. Lovoi unbuckled his seat belt and crept toward the radio operator, fighting off the gravitational effect on such a move. He reached up for the first-aid kit to get some material to wrap around Ligon's thigh to stem the bleeding. Then to add to the confusion of the moment, Major Compton activated the "Bail Out" switch. The wail from this siren was more eerie than the order it screamed. The bomb bay doors were still open and Lovoi wondered why. He looked back into the fuselage and saw the waist gunners and the tail gunner frozen with fear. They did not want to bail out of the stricken aircraft to a certain death over the icy snow-laden mountains.

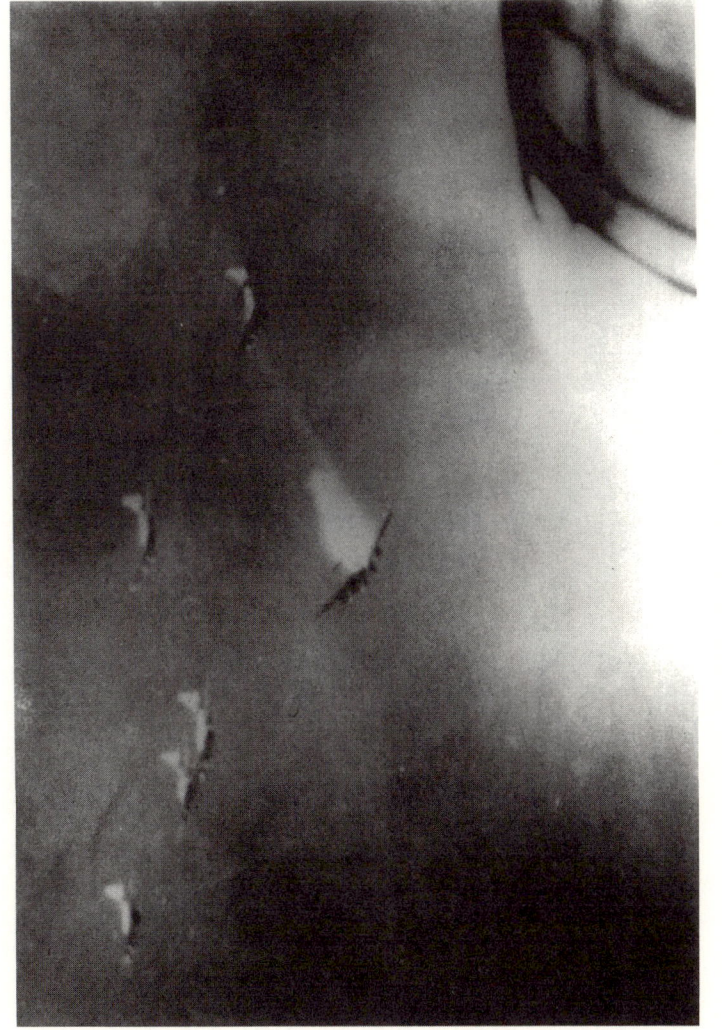

Wichita Belle (ABLE ONE) moments after being hit

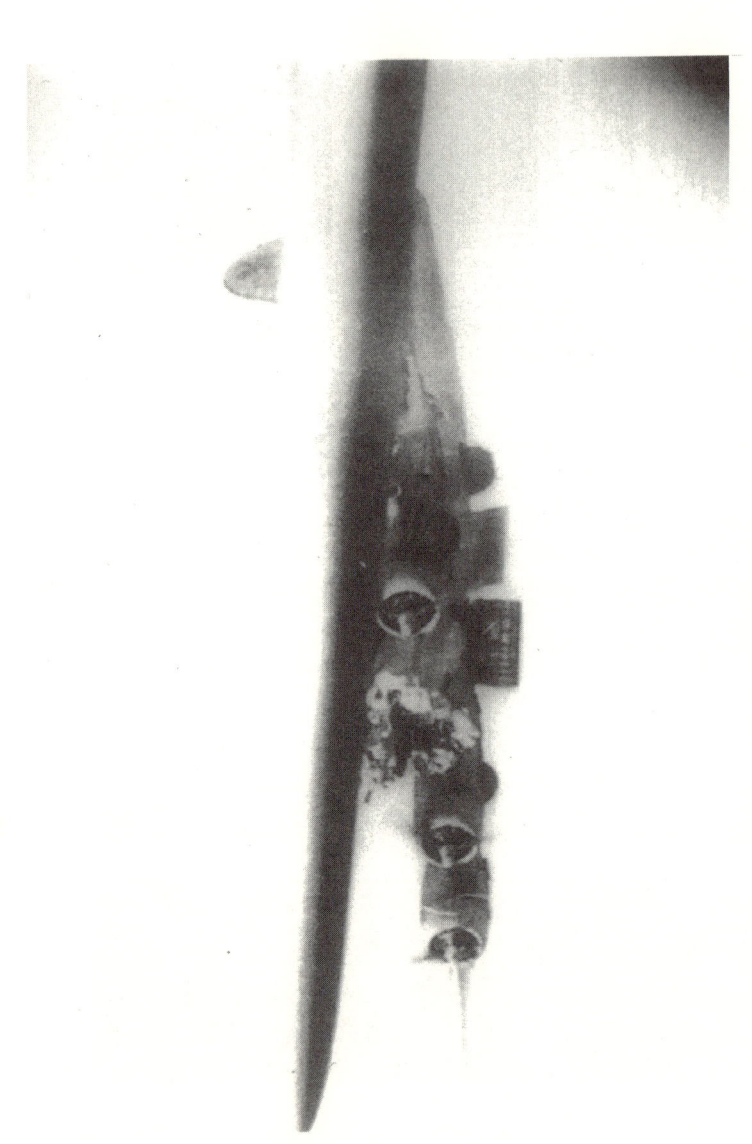

Wichita Belle (ABLE ONE) flak damage

Bombs away!

Innsbruck marshaling yards—November 16, 1944

Lovoi glanced at his altimeter and saw it spinning down through twenty-thousand feet. He transferred his oxygen mask from the system supply to the "walk around" oxygen bottle. This allowed him to move about the B-17 and still have an oxygen supply. He moved toward the open bomb bay and saw that one of the ten bombs had hung up. It was still armed and cradled in its holding shackles. He looked beyond the bomb bay and up into the flight deck. Major Compton was frantically gesturing to him to obey the bail out signal and JUMP!

Lovoi looked down through the open bomb bay and realized that such an escape from the doomed aircraft would only be traded for certain death over the Alps. It would be next summer, if ever, his body would be found. And so he hesitated to obey the command. Instead, he freed the bomb that was hung up in order to remove the danger of an explosion within the bomb bay, and saw it fishtail its way out of the bomb bay and harmlessly explode on a mountainside. Then he unbuckled the oxygen "walk-around" bottle and dropped it through the open bomb bay. The B-17 was flying like a stricken duck. It had spiraled down to seventeen-thousand feet. Two of the plane's engines had been hit, engines number 3 and 4. Engine number 3 was on fire and it was this condition that prompted Major Compton to activate the bail-out siren.

Usually after an engine catches fire, it is followed by an explosion. Engine #4 had to be feathered, that is, its propeller had to be locked to keep it from windmilling. However, due to the skill of Tom Young in bringing the bomber under a measure of control, and the quick action of the Bob Sanford, flight engineer, in activating the fire extinguisher on engine 3, the situation improved tremendously to the point where the "Bail Out" order was rescinded. And not too soon, because by this time Lovoi was sitting on the bomb bay catwalk screwing up his courage to jump. He reasoned that someone had to obey the "Bail Out" order. He was the only officer who might do so. Iorio and Kennedy were having their own problems in the nose section of the plane. Young and Compton were working hard to keep the plane from nose diving to a greedy grave. But just as Lovoi found enough courage to jump, he looked up at the flight deck as if to plead, "Do I really have to?"

Major Compton answered that voiceless question by holding his hand flat up in a "hold it" position. And then he beckoned Lovoi to approach the flight deck. He pulled Lovoi's head close to his mouth and yelled in his ear. "We've got the plane under control, but we're still losing altitude. Quickly, find a map and give me a heading to the Adriatic. If we get that far, we can ditch the aircraft and take our chances on getting picked up by the Navy."

Lovoi did not hesitate a moment. He glanced at the altimeter on the flight panel as he scrambled up to the nose section. The smouldering crippled B-17 was just falling through fifteen-thousand feet. As he stepped into the nose section, the sight that met his eyes was an astonishing one. There was no nose section left. It had been blown off by a direct hit of an anti-aircraft shell over the target. Captain Iorio was lying on his back bleeding from his ankle and moaning in obvious pain. His right foot looked as if it was dangling from what was left of his ankle. Lieutenant Kennedy was administering first aid in the form of a tourniquet around Iorio's right thigh. He had been tightening and loosening it periodically to control the blood flow. Kennedy was using his finger to dip into Iorio's blood pool to record the tourniquet tightening times on Iorio's flight suit. The tourniquet had to be loosened every five minutes.

Lieutenant Lovoi quickly found the appropriate map for their present position. He wiped off Iorio's blood that had splattered over it during the explosion. He looked out the window to try to identify a landmark, any landmark. It was freezing in what was left of nose section. The icy blast kept trying to tear the map from under Lovoi's hands. Actually, he could not feel his hands any more. They were frostbitten and had lost their feeling. At last Lovoi was able to identify a landmark under his right wing with that of a checkpoint on his map. It took but a moment more to measure the angle from that checkpoint, through several mountain passes, and into the Udine Valley of northern Italy. He picked up Kennedy's intercom headset and used it to relay a heading of 165° to the pilot.

The B-17 was now at about the same altitude as the mountain peaks. It would take all the pilots' skills to glide the wounded bomber through the mountain passes, giving up as little altitude as possible for the most distance. And so ABLE ONE continued to glide on a general southeast course into the mountain pass. Major Compton gave the order to throw anything and everything that could be pried loose out of the aircraft. He reopened the bomb bay doors to facilitate the operation. Flak suits, full boxes of machine gun ammunition, oxygen bottles, and yes, even the radar set were all emptied from the wounded warbird.

While the pilots and flight engineer fought to keep the operating engines, #1 and #2, functioning, Lovoi was navigating the B-17 toward a breakthrough from the mountains to the Udine Valley. Kennedy was tending to the wounded, Iorio and Ligon. He had given both of them a morphine shot to ease their pain. Lieutenant Lovoi glanced up at his altimeter and noticed that they had just broken through the eight-thousand-foot level. The glide angle, however, was less obtuse. The mountain peaks were now well above the floundering bomber. As a matter of fact, Lovoi could see the snow mass at the top of the Alps give way to a thin tree line.

The sunlight at this level was nonexistent. The dangerous journey to relative safety was dark and foreboding. A thick overcast blanketed the route. Every unexpected turn might meet with disaster. But good luck was with them adding to the pilots' skill. Suddenly the gliding aircraft broke out of the mountain range's grasp and shook its wings free into the open space and blazing sun of northern Italy. They were still about a mile high and realized they now had something to be optimistic about. If they could maintain enough altitude to reach the coast of the Adriatic Sea, there was a chance they would be picked up by the U.S. Navy speedboats.

This thought had no sooner crossed their collective minds than a barrage of machine-gun bullets pierced their right wing and drew a straight line of dotted holes. Bob Sanford, the flight engineer, jumped up to look through his top turret. He saw a German fighter, an ME-109, tracking the crippled bomber and preparing to blow it out of the sky.

III

Bail Out into Captivity

Major Compton did not hesitate. He hit the "Bail Out" button, and this time everyone in the doomed casket reached for his parachute. Lieutenants Kennedy and Lovoi snapped Captain Iorio's parachute, a chest pack, onto his harness. They half dragged and half carried the wounded bombardier from the nose section to the escape hatch of the B-17. The escape hatch was just below the aircraft's cockpit. Lovoi swung Iorio's legs around so they dropped through the opening of the escape hatch. He then propped the semi-conscious captain in a sitting position on the edge of the escape hatch. He tried not to notice Iorio's shattered foot as it swung back and forth in the slipstream. The cold temperature was a good factor in helping to congeal the flow of blood from his wound.

Lovoi then grasped Iorio's right hand and curled it tightly around the "D-Ring" on his chest pack. The "D-Ring" was like a bolt on a door, its release would send the "pilot" parachute into space. The "pilot" parachute was tied to the main parachute and would pull it out to be deployed. Lovoi put his mouth very close to Iorio's ear so he could be heard above the drone of the engines. He yelled, "Hold tight to the 'D-Ring'. Pull it firmly as you fall free from the plane. I will jump right after you as soon as your parachute opens so I can locate where you might land."

Lovoi was not sure if Iorio understood his message. Iorio's eyes were glazed and his head was slumping forward. But there were no options. Lovoi pushed Iorio out of the B-17 and saw him hurtle earthward. Seconds later he saw the white parachute open and break the fall of his bombardier. Lovoi did not hesitate. He reminded Kennedy to look after Ligon and then rolled out through the escape hatch, clutching his "D-Ring" firmly. The initial rush of cold air almost took his breath away. A few moments later, he pulled on his "D-Ring."

At first, nothing seemed to happen. A feeling of panic stiffened his body. He looked down at his chest pack and began to reach for the "pilot" parachute just under the protective flap. Suddenly his free fall was arrested. He felt as though his plunge was abruptly halted by some giant prehistoric paw that caught his silk parachute and was at arm's length. He felt completely unprotected. He had no sensation of falling. The swinging back and forth abated from a wide motion to a gentle rock. He looked at his wristwatch. It read 2:30 P.M.

The sunlight was blinding. The skies were never bluer. If there wasn't a war going on, this experience might have been pleasantly thrilling. He dared look up at the lifesaving parachute. He was shocked to see that it looked to be the size of a handkerchief, it was so high above him. When he looked down, he got the impression that he was not losing any altitude. He felt that he was just hanging in space at the whim of the giant paw as the giant satisfied its curiosity about this ensnared humanoid. Lovoi looked below and tried to locate Iorio's parachute. He could not find any sign of it. As he followed his "Witchita Belle" under siege, still losing altitude, he spotted three more parachutes opening in sequence. Then the bomber was too low for him to count any more parachutes. He prayed that the rest of the crew escaped the crippled aircraft safely.

The lead radar navigator of the 463rd Bomb Group took a moment to reflect on his situation. The empty feeling in his stomach was new to him. Of course this had never happened to him before. For the first time during his military tour, the matter of life and death loomed large and imminent. He thought he heard something whiz by his ear. The cold silence snugly covered his frost bitten limbs like a wet suit. The sudden change from a noisy aircraft environment to one where the only sound might be the crisp snap of the winter blanket was dramatic. The din from the engines of ABLE ONE had peppered his ear drums for nearly eight steady hours. And there it was again the sound of something whistling over his head. He realized that maybe someone below him was taking shots at him.

He grabbed the parachute shrouds and tried to spill some of the captive air in that "handkerchief" in order to increase his falling velocity. He noticed that one of his parachute's metal harness rings had been sliced. This confirmed that he was a target. He scrunched his frozen body into as small a target as possible, rested his head on the parachute shrouds, and prayed. Now as he approached the earth, he felt as though he was falling too fast. Just as he was about to worry over the impact, his limp body hit the ground. The partially air-filled parachute dragged him on the ground about another fifty feet before coming to a stop.

Lovoi's first reaction was to unbuckle himself from the parachute and find a hiding place. But when he stood erect to do just that, he noticed that he was completely surrounded by a group of dark-uniformed, armed soldiers. They all stared at him but made no threatening gestures. They seemed to be as curious about him as he was of them. Because they appeared to be friendly, Lovoi surmised they were Partisans, a band of hill dwellers who tried to help parachuting Allied crews to reach safe havens. The Partisans were from Allied bases, and dropped by parachute at night and hid in the mountains and hills of Italy and Yugoslavia. Their job was to look for parachuting Allied airmen and reach them when they hit the ground before the Germans or Italians did. Then they would whisk them away to a mountain hideout and eventually sneak them back across the enemy lines to some Allied station for repatriation.

Unfortunately for Lovoi, this band of soldiers were not Partisans. They were members of the Italian Blackshirt Army. Not knowing this fact, the lieutenant began to speak to them in his very broken Italian dialect. He effectively said, "Let's get out of here before we are discovered." But when they did not react to this suggestion, he began to realize his mistake. One of the soldiers pointed his rifle at him and demanded his flight jacket, his chronometer, his escape kit with all the goodies in it, his 0.45 caliber side arm, and flight gloves. Then two of the men flanked him, firmly grasped his upper arms, and walked him out of the field where he landed and onto a dirt road just about twenty-five yards ahead. The dirt road was a short one and led to a secondary highway.

The fact that the dirt road was lined with civilian women, most of them sobbing, was very disturbing to Lovoi. While he was trying to figure out why they were weeping, he caught the sight of an angry soldier rushing toward him with rifle butt raised and ready to strike. Lovoi could not defend himself because he was being held by two other soldiers. He did manage to squirm his body around enough to parry the blow with the nape of his neck. Other soldiers quickly restrained the raging soldier and kept him from doing any further damage. Lovoi felt the trickle of hot blood as it seeped down the back of his neck and into his flight suit. The soldiers spoke with one another in excited tones.

Lovoi could not understand any of the conversations. There seemed to be some sort of delay in transporting him to wherever he was to be interrogated. The men kept looking up the highway as though they were expecting someone or something. They were in communication with someone by radio. By the side of the road was a jeep-like vehicle with a small wooden cart in tow. Lovoi wondered if that was to be the means of transportation.

At last the reason for the delay became evident. An Italian soldier was coming into view from a wooded area and he had a heavy burden on his back. As he came closer, Lovoi was dismayed to see that it was Captain Iorio being borne toward the waiting band of enemy soldiers. He was conscious but in obvious pain. He was dumped into the wooden cart behind the jeep-like vehicle where he lay motionless. Lovoi was ordered to get in the cart beside Iorio. The two men looked at each other stoically. They did not dare to show any happy emotion lest that act would infuriate the soldiers.

Again there seemed to be a delay. One of the soldiers was speaking loudly over his radio again. Lovoi did not understand any of that conversation either. But within a few minutes, another group of soldiers came through the woods. This time they had in hand a man dressed in civilian clothes. His face reflected English features. They ordered him into the rear seat of the Italian jeep.

Lovoi surmised that this unfortunate prisoner was indeed a Partisan and that his fate was grim. All this commotion was followed by the arrival of a German jeep.

Into enemy hands

It contained a driver and three German officers. They immediately began to speak to the Italian soldiers and occasionally gestured toward the two American flyers. The Italian soldiers raised their voices as if in protest. It was difficult to perceive what the nature of the argument was. And then it became apparent that the German officers wanted to take the prisoners into their custody for interrogation. Apparently a compromise was worked out because the Italian jeep, followed by the German jeep, headed for a destination.

On the way Lovoi tried to converse with Iorio concerning his physical condition. But Iorio was too weak to hold conversation. He seemed to alternate between a state of semi-consciousness and pain. He had lost a lot of blood. The makeshift bandage that Kennedy had wrapped around the wound was soiled and loose. Lovoi put his arm around his shoulders and wondered if he was about to lose his brave bombardier.

The trip to their destination took about fifteen minutes. The sun had set and the skies were now gray. The dropping temperature was bone chilling. Neither of the flyers was dressed for the occasion. Lovoi cradled Iorio and shared whatever body heat he could. But soon the two jeeps came to a halt. Lovoi was ordered out. He barely had time to bid farewell to Iorio. The Italian jeep sped off as soon as Lovoi disengaged himself from the wooden trailer. It disappeared around a bend in the dirt road of the Italian military camp. Iorio was taken to a nearby farmhouse. Although he was still semi-conscious, the shock of his injuries seemed to shroud the physical pain throughout his body. Shortly he was unceremoniously dumped on the dirt floor of an empty silo. He was given a small meal consisting of pasta and beans. He was provided with a shawl for a blanket, and then the door of the silo closed with a bang, leaving him with his misery for the remainder of the evening.

On the next morning his cold and wounded body was transported to a rather large Italian villa and deposited in the basement of the structure where he was again left alone. He wondered. What was next?

Within several minutes he was greeted by a German officer who introduced himself as a doctor. He examined the wounded parts of Iorio's body. He meticulously disengaged Iorio's bloodied flight suit from his shattered right ankle. He cleaned the gaping wound and bound it with bandage material. The doctor then removed a piece of shrapnel from Iorio's left eye and several small pieces from his back and thighs. He decided not to remove the piece that had penetrated the back of his head. By this time Iorio could stand the pain no longer. The doctor then injected him with a shot of morphine and Iorio lapsed into unconsciousness. When he came to sometime later, he found himself in a cold and damp moving railroad box car. As he focused his eyes on his surroundings, he was aware that he had company. Another injured flyer was lying several feet from him. Iorio dragged himself toward that figure who was also semi-conscious. In a moment, Iorio recognized his traveling companion. It was Tom Ligon, his wounded radio operator!

Lovoi's arrival drew a small crowd. Curious Italian soldiers gathered around him for a firsthand look. Moments later he was whisked away into a very large tent. He was ushered in, followed by the Italian guards and the German officers.

Lieutenant Lovoi looked around to get his bearings. Straight ahead was a large desk with several piles of papers and a briefcase. Behind the desk stood a medium-built Italian officer, hands fisted, leaning on the desk.

His chair was pushed back out of the way behind him. The tent was well lighted and reasonably heated. There were several rows of file cabinets next to the desk. This tent looked to be headquarters in a rear army post. There were several chairs scattered around the room. Several staff, who were milling about at first, abruptly came to a quiet standstill as Lovoi was escorted toward the main desk. The German officers, the Italian officer, and the American prisoner were framed in a dramatic triangle.

The Italian officer pressed forward and addressed his prisoner as Lieutenant. His questions were asked in the Italian language. Full name? What was the target of today's mission? Where is your home base located? Although Lovoi did understand the gist of these questions, he acted as though he did not understand a word of the interrogator's tirade. He realized that if he gave the impression that he had any "Italian" blood in him that he would be considered a traitor and not a prisoner of war. The Italian definition of nationality concerns itself with "blood lines" as opposed to the American definition citing "birthplace."

After Lovoi had shrugged his shoulders as the international act of incomprehension after each question, the interrogator became livid. Raising his voice, he threw his clenched fist into his prisoner's face and said in his native language, "If I hit you with one of these, you would understand me, no?" Lovoi shrunk from the fist and the danger. It seemed that he was about to get roughed up to satisfy the Italian officer's frustration.

But just then, the German officers stepped between the interrogator and his prisoner and quietly but firmly dissuaded him from his cowardly act. Even though Lovoi could not make any sense of the conversation, he concluded that the German officers had convinced the interrogator that Lovoi had to be interrogated by German intelligence in the belief that they could educe valuable military information from him.

With a parting evil glance, the Italian officer ordered the guards to take Lovoi away to a secure location. If looks could kill, Lovoi would have been slain on the spot by the contemptuous expression on his captor's face. Lovoi felt as though he had just dodged a bullet, perhaps the first of many more to come. He was brusquely escorted out of this main tent and into a smaller one just a few yards down a narrow grassy path. The cold Italian evening spread its chill over the army post. One of the guards disappeared for a while but returned with a thin blanket for Lovoi to use to keep him from freezing. The blanket had seen better days, but Lovoi was grateful to have it. The holding tent was bare of furniture. The floor was grass.

Lovoi sat down, pulled the blanket around his shoulders, and rubbed his arms and legs in order to maintain maximum blood circulation. He felt exhausted. He could not believe what was happening to him. He reviewed the last twelve hours or so in his mind. He wished he could wake up and admit he had a nightmare. But reality kept staring him in his face. Was he not feeling the cold and hunger? Had he not just been separated from his wounded bombardier? Were those not enemy soldiers' voices he could hear just outside his tent? And what about the future—was there any?

He closed his eyes and lay on his side. His thoughts transcended to 104 Hancock Street, Cambridge, Massachusetts. How would his family, especially his parents, absorb the shock of the "Missing In Action" telegram from the War Department? He prayed that the "Prisoner of War" telegram would not be too far behind.

He must have fallen asleep, because the next thing he remembered was being shaken awake by two German guards who motioned him to exit the tent and walk between them to a waiting German half-ton personnel vehicle. Of course he obeyed. The wind chill reminded him that he was woefully unprepared for this climate. To add to his temperature woes, he was relieved of his warm flying boots when he reached the vehicle. They were replaced by a used pair of army shoes, which were not nearly as warm as his boots were. But he was in no position to argue or to negotiate. He silently complied with the swap. He supposed it could have been worse. He had heard of cases where the confiscated boots were not replaced at all in order to discourage thoughts of escape.

He sat in the back of the truck in a huddled position with the blanket around his shoulders. The two guards sat next to him. The cab of the truck was enclosed by a metal driver's compartment. The rear of the truck was enclosed by a canvas weather protector. The driver started the vehicle's engine and set it to idle. The German guards were chatting with each other. Lovoi was trying to keep warm. It seemed that the next move was "on hold." Minutes passed. The guards became restless. They jumped out of the truck and lit a cigarette, which they shared. Lovoi estimated that the waiting dragged on to well over one-half an hour.

It ended abruptly when a German officer arrived and exchanged military salutes with the guards. Lovoi guessed his rank was that of a major. He thought he could make out officer's insignia on the epaulets of the officer's army coat. When all four passengers were seated in the truck, the driver put the transmission in gear and urged it into motion with the gas pedal. The vehicle moved slowly within the confines of the camp. It stopped at the sentry gate to be inspected by the Italian Military Police. When the MP's were satisfied as to the identification of the human cargo, the journey to "somewhere" had begun. Within a few minutes, they reached a highway and the vehicle accelerated to a high speed. Its headlights were partially blacked out, making it difficult for Allied pilots, flying night sorties, to see and to attack.

Lovoi did recognize a road sign as they entered the ramp leading to the highway. It read Conegliano. He remembered this checkpoint from the many scans he executed on his maps during his now twenty-nine missions. It was a small town thirty miles north of Venice. So it became somewhat obvious to him that they were headed north to Germany. As the trip progressed, the temperature got colder. The wind seemed to come from all directions. His ears popped as the outside air pressure fell. These clues confirmed that they were heading north into the foothills of the Italian Alps. As if to reconfirm this fact, it began to snow lightly.

None of the passengers spoke during this phase of the trip. Each man was deep in his own thoughts. For the first time since his arrival in Italy, Lovoi felt the early pangs of anxiety and depression. He had never been so out of control over his actions as he was at this time. His black-and-white world was beginning to take on some shades of gray. He was beginning to pay his share of the price for the preservation of freedom.

It seemed about an hour later, when the vehicle entered the outskirts of an urban area. The snow was falling more heavily at this point. Lovoi tried to look for signs of his whereabouts as the truck slowed to a speed consistent with city driving. The truck finally stopped by the side of a street that had multi-storied buildings abutting it. The driver got out of the truck and came to the open rear.

He spoke to the major briefly and then the two of them left the scene. While they were gone, the two guards jumped off the tail end and lighted up cigarettes.

From where Lovoi was sitting, he got a view of the street and some of the stores that lined it. He was able to read the sign on one of the stores. It read Restorante Bolzano. Bolzano is a large industrial city in northern Italy situated in the foothills of the Alps and marks the southern end of the Brenner Pass. The Brenner Pass is the most accessible route between Italy and Austria. It has an elevation of about five thousand feet. Its northern end is the city of Innsbruck, Austria. As the conditions began to reveal themselves to Lovoi, he nervously realized that the destination of this small party might well be Innsbruck. His heart pumped a little faster at this possibility. He did not have long to wait. The major and the driver returned with a cardboard box of sandwiches and hot ersatz coffee. He was given half a sandwich and a cardboard cup of black coffee. The food hit the spot. Lieutenant Lovoi savored every bit of the boloney sandwich on black bread. It was his first experience with black bread. All he could say about it was that it was different. The sugarless coffee washed it down.

Within minutes of the last bites and swallows, the vehicle was on its way. It was a black cold night. The falling snow could be seen now and then as they passed by the shaded lights of the very light oncoming traffic. And then they were at the beginning of the Brenner Pass. The ride through the Brenner Pass was very bumpy and windy. It was bumpy because the road through it had been bombed on many occasions to cut off ground traffic between Austria and Italy. It was windy because the Brenner Pass' geological makeup had varying distances in width. This fact causes ever-changing air pressure within the relative narrow passage, thus the blustery winds.

And so the truck made it through the Alps and into Austrian territory. The highway leading from the Pass went west. The snowfall had abated on this side of the mountain range. But the temperature felt colder. Lovoi's ears popped again as the air pressure change affected his ear drums. He felt his stomach tighten as the truck picked up speed toward its destination. At last his worst fears gripped him and left a sick feeling in his gut. From his position in the truck, he looked for road signs. At one of the crossroads, the truck slowed down to take a turn. At the corner of the turn was a road sign barely visible in the dark night. Suddenly, he felt his heart pump faster. It read "Innsbruck-5km"!

IV

A Fruitful Journey North

It was now almost midnight, twelve hours since ABLE ONE had dropped its devastation on the marshaling yards on the outskirts of Innsbruck; twelve hours since the retaliatory enemy anti-aircraft fire mortally crippled ABLE ONE with those brave men in it; twelve hours since Lovoi's parachute opened up, only to spare him for enemy capture.

The vehicle raced on for about fifteen more minutes and slowly decelerated as though it was nearing its destination. A sharp right turn brought it into a railroad station whose main building exhibited an identification sign, which read "Innsbruck." The building was badly damaged. It was windowless, most of the roof was caved in, several walls were leveled, and parts of it were still smoking. Repair crews were piling the debris into manageable piles of glass, bricks, plaster, and wood. There were no lights. Makeshift electrical wiring was used to transfer power from an emergency generator to the few scattered bulbs within what was left of the building.

The vehicle stopped squarely in front of this building. It used to be a passenger terminal. As a matter of fact, several hundred soldiers and civilians were milling about within what was still under part of the roof. They appeared to be waiting for a train. The rest of the station within Lovoi's vision did not fare any better. Twisted rail lines were poking up from the ground. Maintenance crews were repairing them as quickly as possible in order to allow the trains to move through Innsbruck. Distant sirens confirmed the fact that some fires were still smouldering. A pall of black dust covered most of the railroad yard. Lovoi could see some damaged engines off their tracks. Freight cars were damaged and overturned. Huge craters dotted the area in haphazard design. Lovoi was shocked to see how much devastation the 463rd Bomb Group created on one raid. This was the first time he actually saw the incredible results of his military profession. Yes, it would be a while before the station would be able to support the Nazi armies. Lovoi wondered what the total cost in Allied lives and enemy lives amounted to, as a result of this raid.

As soon as the truck stopped, the German major hopped out of the tail section, bade the two guards farewell, saluted them in a crisp motion, and without even glancing at Lovoi, disappeared into the crowd that was waiting for its train. The two guards then bade the driver good-bye and escorted Lovoi between them into the damaged waiting room. By now the weather was well below freezing. Occasionally a gust of frigid air broke through as if to remind the human assembly that there was a war going on, and not to get too comfortable. The blast nipped and bit each person in its path, let itself through the damaged building, and searched for other victims to nip and bite.

The guards kept a casual eye on Lovoi. They did not act as though they were guarding a prisoner of war. The lieutenant was grateful for that. His fears that he would be recognized as a bomber crew member were well founded. A good number of Allied airmen had met their fate at the hands of a crowd with ropes and pitchforks. The cold must have numbed everyone because no one paid any attention to Lovoi. The crowd was relatively silent. They paced like programmed zombies. Everyone was waiting for a train to arrive. It did not matter that the tracks were still under repair. It seemed the crowd was used to the waiting. They knew that the train would eventually arrive. The cold was so bitter that several military types decided to build a fire in the middle of the roofless waiting room. There were plenty of wood pieces for fuel. The floor was made of tile over cement. The fire could be contained in the event of wind gusts.

The idea seemed like a good one at first. As the fire grew, its heat was being felt by the passengers who were in the abutting areas. And for awhile even Lovoi's frostbitten hands and feet began to respond. But the smoke from the fire soon filled the room, finding every one of the waiting passengers causing a symphony of choking sounds. The coughing grew louder and louder until the soldiers who started the fire were convinced that they should put it out. And so the moment of warmth was quickly replaced with several hours of continued cold and windy weather.

The question of escape crept into Lovoi's mind at this stage of his captivity. He reasoned that he could easily melt his way into the milling crowd and not be noticed for some time. The night was very dark. The overcast that ABLE ONE bombed through was still hanging around. Most conditions for escape were favorable. However, Lovoi was not dressed for such an ordeal. He could not speak German, and his hands and feet were frostbitten beyond sensation. Even if he were able to escape from Innsbruck, his only salvation would be Switzerland, which was several hundred miles to the west and over the frozen Alps that separated Switzerland from Austria. He decided against the attempt at this time and to wait for a better opportunity.

It must have been past three o'clock in the morning. He was so cold and tired that he sat on the cement floor of the waiting room and slumped against what was left of the wall. He dozed off in a fitful slumber, waking up each time his head slipped down along the wall. It was a losing battle. There was no way he could get comfortable enough to rest his weary body. The reality of his hopeless situation began to take over his mind. He was miserable. He was scared. How could this happen to him? He closed his eyes and blocked out the visual disaster scene around him. He whispered a prayer and begged for help.

Dawn was beginning to streak its arrival on the eastern horizon. It was a gray beginning. A thick layer of stratus clouds prevented the sun from spewing its warmth over the Austrian foothills. The waiting passengers started to move slowly in several directions. It was bitter cold. The maintenance crews looked very tired as they mopped up the last of their track repairs. In the distance an engine wailed its warning to anyone who might be on its track as it slowly inched its way in front of the waiting room.

Soon everyone in the room was awake and pressed closer to the track in anticipation of the train's arrival. They were not disappointed. The huge black engine with puffs of steam leaking from its control conduits crept to its allocated position, pulling what seemed to be an endless number of old passenger cars. Even before it came to a complete stop, the passengers were crawling into it and claiming their seats. With sighs of relief, they slumped into their seats and waited for the next move.

Lovoi was ushered by his guards into one of the passenger cars and directed to sit on one of the seats. The guards pulled the backrest of the seat in front of Lovoi and sat facing him. When the train finally began to move, the guards were facing in the direction of travel and Lovoi was facing backward to the direction of travel. He was too tired to contemplate the situation. He pulled his blanket up over his shoulders, rested his head on the armrest of the seat, and was soon fast asleep.

When he woke up, the train was stopped. The guards were nowhere in sight. For a moment he panicked, but just for a moment. He looked out the window and saw both guards standing nearby smoking a cigarette. As a matter of fact, many of the passengers were off the train standing by and smoking cigarettes. A few of them were eating snacks and conversing. The guards noticed Lovoi looking out the window and waved to him. Then they beckoned for him to come outside and join them. Although he did not like the cold blast of air that whipped past him, he did as he was told. The sun was out, poking its way around a few high cumulus clouds.

Lovoi noticed that the engine was located on a spur track and the train was well hidden by a large grove of trees. This day's weather was conductive to low-level Allied strafing attacks. During these conditions very little traffic moved throughout the German territory. The risk of being destroyed was too great. And so the traffic had to wait until the weather conditions made it all but impossible for the Allied fighter bombers to fly, or the traffic had to wait for the cover of darkness.

The two guards spoke briefly to the train conductor and began walking from the hidden spur track over to a large field of snow-filled acreage. They ordered Lovoi to walk with them. Lovoi's heart began to beat faster. He

53

wondered what was up. Why did the three of them head into an open field of frozen tundra? The cold wind accompanied them as they made their way. Then they came upon a small hill. They marched up the hill and reached a small mesa. The snow was almost knee deep. Lovoi's hands and feet were not seriously affected, they were already frostbitten. But now his face was beginning to freeze as the wind continued its harassing behavior, looking for an opening between Lovoi's blanket and shirt collar.

He was still wondering what was the meaning of this brisk walk when he spied a farm house in the distance. It sat up on a naked hill surrounded by an open animal shed and a silo. The dark gray smoke rising from its chimney was evidence that there was a fire in the house somewhere, either in a fireplace or in a kitchen stove. The sight of their destination encouraged new life into Lovoi's weary legs. The three men approached the front doorway and stamped the snow from their legs and shoes.

Almost simultaneously the door opened and revealed a very large handsome woman standing between its jamb. She wore a warm smile, a clean cardigan sweater, a full apron tied at the waist, and an ankle-length winter dress. The two guards pushed Lovoi in front of them and greeted the lady with several German phrases. They nodded and smiled as they entered the large kitchen, closing the door behind them. The warm room was a welcome treat, but it was the aroma of rural cooking that particularly excited Lovoi's appetite. The guards seemed to be explaining to the Frau that they were escorting a prisoner to an interrogation center and that they were being delayed due to good weather. The Frau animatedly nodded her head and beckoned the three visitors to be seated at a large wooden table in the center of the kitchen. The guards placed their rifles against the wall near the doorway, removed their army coats and hats, and sat at the table. Lovoi removed his thin blanket and soft military cap and sat at the table also.

The lady of the house bustled back and forth, carrying dishes from the pantry to the table, a loaf of black bread, and three well used but clean cotton napkins. Then she stayed by the stove where she was stirring and cooking a large pot of vegetable soup with a small amount of beef in it. The two guards talked with each other. Lovoi glanced about the room, taking in the unusual decor of a German farmhouse kitchen.

It was relatively large, perhaps twenty feet by thirty feet. Three of the four walls included windows, which were curtained with flowered drapes pulled back with swag ties. The center entrance doorway was bordered by a seat-type coat rack with a mirrored back and an ornamental seat with a lift-up top. The floor was constructed with wide hard wooden boards that wore a dull clean finish. Several area rugs were placed within the kitchen, one under the table, one in the doorway, and one in the far part of the kitchen, away from the iron stove. Besides the kitchen table and its five wooden chairs, the only furniture that Lovoi could see comprised of a couple of sofas about the size of love seats, an arm chair, and a credenza against one of the walls. On the wall opposite the doorway was a straight stairway, which led up to a second floor. It was an open-type stairway with crude wooden bannisters on both sides of the steps.

Just as Lovoi was beginning to feel the pangs of his hunger within his stomach, the Frau carried the pot of food to the table, set it on a metal plate, and ladled some of its contents into the three cupped dishes, one for each of the afternoon visitors. The lieutenant could see the steam rise above his plate. He marveled at the manner in which the Frau picked up the loaf of bread, cuddled it to her breast, and with a sharp knife sliced it neatly into several pieces, all the while not inflicting a scratch. She placed the neatly severed slices on a large napkin in the center of the table and gestured the visitors to begin their meal. The three men looked up at her with questioning glances. "Ach!" she muttered, as she scrambled her way to the pantry, retrieved three soup spoons, and placed them triumphantly before her diners. The Germans laughed softly at this performance, a common one on many occasions. Even Lovoi had to smile through his misery at the incident.

The soup was delicious. Lovoi tried to eat his meal at a pace consistent with the two guards. He really had no problem. The guards were feeding like there was no tomorrow. So Lovoi showed good manners by being the last of the three to finish his meal. One of the guards looked at his timepiece. He then had a brief conversation with the Frau. The result of the conversation was that the three visitors would spend additional time at the farm house. The Frau faced the stairway and called a name. Lovoi did not understand it, but it sounded like "Lisa."

Almost immediately a young, slim, neatly dressed girl opened the door at the top of the stairway and proceeded to come down into the kitchen. She had jet-black hair and fair skin. Her dark eyes were averted from the visitors and rested on the face of the Frau. She was asked to clean up the kitchen table and wash the dishes. One of the guards sat at the table with the Frau while the other guard escorted Lovoi up the stairs and into a narrow corridor. At the end of the corridor, there was a bathroom. Along the corridor there were three closed doors.

Lovoi was escorted to the room at the opposite end of the bathroom. The guard opened the door and motioned Lovoi to enter. It was a small bedroom with a single neatly made bed. The woolen bedspread and the pillow cover matched the hooked rug on the floor at the foot of the bed. The guard gestured for Lovoi to lie down and rest. He turned around and left him alone. The prisoner did not need to be asked twice. He dropped his body on top of the bed, fully clothed, and almost instantly fell asleep. He did not know how long he slept.

When he was shaken awake by the guard, the room was dark. He felt very tired. Again, as the reality of his situation sank in, he felt very depressed. He still could not cope with the issue of his captivity. The two men entered the corridor. It too was dark with just a dim shadow of light coming through the open doorway at the head of the stairs. The guard pointed to the bathroom at the end of the corridor. Lovoi took the offer and walked into the bathroom, closed the door, and relieved himself. Several minutes later he emerged from the bathroom and faced an empty corridor. He walked toward the open doorway that led down the stairs to the kitchen. But before reaching the doorway, he saw the middle door opening. Just as he reached it, the young Lisa came out of the room. The corridor was too narrow for two people to use except in single file. The two young bodies gently collided. Lovoi blurted, "Excuse me." The young lady's face was close to his. He could see that she was very pretty.

She drew back to let him go by. As he did, she reached for his hand. He hesitated for a moment and questioningly looked at her. She quickly placed a small hard object in the palm of his hand, turned away, and disappeared back into the room from which she appeared. Lovoi quickly put the object into his pants pocket and climbed down the stairway to meet with the guards and the Frau. They were bidding each other good-bye. Lovoi's knees were shaking from his recent unexpected encounter. He was worried that his demeanor might uncover his excitement.

The three visitors exited the farm house and retraced their steps on the path to where the train was located. The night was dark but with just enough light from a cloud-hidden moon for guiding them on their return. Lovoi dared a glance back to the farm house just after the Frau closed its front door. He looked up at the nearest second-floor window and saw a young face staring in his direction. He thought it was Lisa. He dared not wave for fear of getting her in trouble.

When the trio finally reached the train, it was pitch black outside. This was perfect traveling weather. As if to underscore this fact, the engine blasted its whistle to alert the milling passengers to board the train. Lovoi and his guards did just that. After settling down on his appointed seat and pulling his blanket around his upper body, Lovoi reached into his pants pocket and pulled out the unexpected gift from Lisa. While the guards were engaged in their own conversation, Lovoi took a quick peek under his blanket at his gift. It was a small hard apple!

A heart-stopping moment

V

For You the War Is Over

Lieutenant Joseph Lovoi spent the second day of his captivity as a passenger on a train that was generally headed north, that was unheated and unlighted, that made many stops varying from just minutes to several hours, and whose human cargo kept redistributing itself with each stop. During several of the longer stops, one of the guards would disappear for awhile and return with lukewarm ersatz coffee, slices of margerined black bread, and some cheese pieces. The guards shared some of this picnic with Lovoi. He noticed that with each stop the civilian passenger numbers grew while the military passengers diminished in number. This meant that the train was indeed well into the heartland of the German Reich.

Lovoi's thoughts of escape seemed more hopeless now than ever. He began to put more emphasis on how to survive the captivity and less emphasis on how to analyze it. Survival had to be his number one priority. To support this priority, he realized that it would take all of his physical stamina and lots more courage than he had at the moment. He knew he had to develop a courage that would preserve his very life.

The train was traveling at a moderate pace throughout the second night of his captivity. The rhythmic metallic music that came from the collision of its wheels against the uneven iron rail, helped lull Lovoi into a state of inactive thoughtfulness. Yes, he went home for a while to see how his parents and siblings were responding to his recent MIA category. He did not like what he saw. But he was helpless to alleviate the demoralizing effects. He sensed that all of them, except his pious mother, were thinking the unthinkable. He then thought of his girl back home, Rosalie Browne. How was she taking it? Hopefully she and his family were supportive of each other. He wondered if his personal belongings at the bomber base in Foggia would be sent home to his parents. He remembered Lucia, his Italian friend who worked at the Red Cross in Foggia. What was her reaction when his ABLE ONE B-17 failed to return?

Finally the train was slowing down as though it were approaching a stop. Lovoi squirmed his body in every which way to stretch his aching limbs and wake up his circulation. He pulled the blanket a bit tighter around his collar. The train slowed to a crawl. It was entering a multi-track station of large proportions that had seen better days. Several trains were already stationed on their designated tracks. There were lots of passenger cars and freight cars just loosely located and not attached to engines. And now the train was moving alongside of a platform. It slowed down and inched its way toward the terminal center.

Lovoi could see people walking briskly along the platform. They were both men and women with a scattering of military personnel. All were well dressed, belying the devastation seen in the disastrous wreckage within what was left of the walls and roof of this terminal. Lovoi craned his neck to try to find any identifying signs on this station. At last the train stopped. The guards motioned Lovoi to remain seated. The remaining coach passengers made their way to the exit doors and

61

disappeared. Lovoi continued to scan the bombed terminal and finally located a sign post with a dirty white
panel across it. It read, "Frankfurt (Am Main)."

The station looked as if it had been visited by a hurri-
cane. The buildings that were left standing were severely
damaged by bombs and fire. The terminal had some walls
standing and partial roofs hanging on. Repair and maintenance crews were on the job trying to clear the twisted
mess so that trains and passengers could navigate safely.
Traffic within the bomb-damaged terminal was thin and
slow. The passengers however, were well dressed. They
were carrying bags, valises, and briefcases. Their manner
was businesslike and brisk. They acted as though they
were used to these chaotic conditions.

About fifteen minutes after the train carrying Lovoi
and his two guards stopped, the trio exited the passenger
car and headed toward a remote part of what was left of
the station. Within minutes they were met by a group
of similar travelers, two German guards and four Allied
prisoners. The four guards began to exchange words and
papers to one another's satisfaction. Lovoi felt mixed
emotions; thankfulness for the friendly company, and
sorrow for the obvious fate of his friendly company. The
prisoners were not allowed to exchange words. But their
facial expressions said volumes. The four new friends
were dressed in American uniforms that had seen better
days. All five prisoners looked cold, grimy, unshaven, and
extremely tired.

Suddenly two of the four guards, Lovoi's escorts,
waved farewell and disappeared into the morning haze.
The remaining guards positioned the prisoners single file
and then stationed themselves, one in front of the file
and one in the rear of the file. They were armed with
rifles. Their orders were to take the prisoners to the bus

station nearby. The conspicuous group of seven soldiers quick stepped its way out of the railroad station and onto the urban street. The guards appeared nervous as they urged their prisoners to move swiftly.

At first, no one seemed to notice this strange formation, but soon scattered civilians began to take second looks at it. Within several minutes, some of the civilians formed a small group and shouted epithets as the formation continued to move ahead. The small gathering began to take on the numbers of a crowd. The shouting became louder and louder.

The crowd began to close the distance between the quick stepping soldiers and itself. The Americans realized that they were in a very precarious position. Lovoi recalled stories of how the civilian population occasionally managed to get hold of Allied prisoners and put them to death. In some cases death came slowly from the result of beatings or hanging. On their way from the station to the bus stop, the group of seven passed by a high brick wall. Here the two guards halted the quick step and ordered the five prisoners to stand against the brick wall in close formation. They then took their position in front of the prisoners and faced the menacing crowd. They shouted to the crowd that these prisoners had valuable military information, which would be extracted from them by the German Intelligence Office at the interrogation center.

But the crowd was too incited by now. They even had a youthful leader who kept repeating such phrases as "air gangsters" and *"kinder* killers." Their bloody appetites had been whetted, and they were not about to give up their prey. The mob drew closer. The guards shouted "Halt" and quickly dropped to one knee, leveling their rifles at the mob. The shouting stopped and the front line of the mob was glued in its tracks. The guards took advantage of this momentary confusion and cocked the triggers. That did it! The screaming mob disbursed in every direction. The youthful leader, however, stood his ground. He glared at the two aiming guards and called them traitors. Slowly he retreated and the seven soldiers were back on their way to the bus station. The rest of the journey was without incident.

The bus station had seen its share of Allied bomb damage also. One small building was left standing. Its parking area was littered with damaged vehicles that would carry no more passengers. One of the guards entered the building and spoke with the clerk at the desk. After a short conversation, he came out and informed the other guard that they were to wait a short time for a bus to arrive that would transport the seven passengers to the interrogation center at Wetzlar, a small town about thirty miles away from Frankfurt. It was bitter cold. The noon sun had little warming effect on the prisoners of war. As Lovoi relived the events of the last hour, he knew he had dodged another bullet. He wondered if the two guards would really have fired upon their own countrymen to save the lives of their enemy.

Eventually, a bus arrived and stopped in front of the bus station. The driver turned off the ignition, went into the office, and exchanged papers with the clerk. After a short conversation, he emerged, opened the bus door, and invited the party of seven to enter the vehicle and be seated. The five prisoners were instructed to seat themselves in the first three double-seated rows while the two guards sat in the fifth row, one on each side of the bus.

The driver was the last one to enter. He sat on the driver's seat and tried to start the vehicle. The engine sputtered and coughed but refused to start. Then the driver primed the engine with some sort of choke control, waited a few moments, and tried to start the engine again. This time it kicked in and with a cloud of black exhaust, it settled down to an even idle. The driver then put the transmission in forward gear and the bus was on its way to the interrogation center. The ride took about forty-five minutes. It was uneventful except for the bouncing and rocking action caused by the deep potholes and debris-cluttered streets.

The passengers knew that they had reached their destination when the bus slowed down to negotiate a tight ninety-degree turn in a long narrow driveway. The big iron gate was open and a guard was standing beside it. The driveway was in good repair, and the bus had no trouble reaching the portico just in front of a large oak door whose planks were held together with black iron fasteners. The door was a double-hung Palladian type, each half boasting a large black iron handle with which to open and close it. The building that this doorway opened into was a three-storied government, gray block type with large double hung windows along the front on the first two stories, and equal number of A-frame dormers, which accented the third story. The grounds surrounding the structure were covered with several feet of snow and ice. The few trees that lined the driveway showed some white and green mixture in color, the white being snow and the green being pine needles. The high snow piles along each side of the driveway indicated that several recent snowstorms had paid a visit to Wetzlar.

When the bus stopped, one-half of the big double-oak door leading into the building opened. Two neatly uniformed German military types emerged and waited in the portico until the bus was empty and its occupants standing silently in some kind of formation. The two German guards who accompanied the five prisoners to this interrogation center walked up to one of the uniformed military types, snapped a "Heil Hitler" salute, and handed him a large envelope with documents enclosed. The German officer perused them for a moment and then called the names of the five POW's, pausing after each name to look up and take note of the POW who answered to his name.

Then after a short conversation with the two German guards, he shouted to the POW's, in clear English, "Follow me." And they did. The bus driver and the two German guards left the scene. Lovoi did not look forward to this next phase of his captivity. He felt that he was getting closer and closer to the time when he would either learn his fate, or at least have his fate decided based upon what happened at this interrogation center.

The POW's followed the German officer into a large square room with a high vaulted ceiling. The second German officer brought up the rear of the single file and closed the door to this room after everyone was inside. Lovoi looked around. The room was painted a dull grayish-white. The four walls were decorated with sconces, which provided the light for this room. The wooden molding around the ceiling was hound's tooth design, giving the room a very formal appearance. The furniture was made up of file cabinets, several desks, and half a dozen tables. Most of the desks and tables had papers and briefcases on their tops. The largest of the desks was the one at the opposite end of the room from its entrance. It was complemented by a high-back leather swivel chair.

The meeting was short and military-like. A German officer, who spoke perfect English, told the POW's that they would be put into solitary confinement until it was clear to the German authorities that they were indeed true military captives and not Allied spies who were parading as POW's. It was suggested that if the POW's were cooperative at the interrogation session, which were to begin on the next day, their stay in solitary would be short. If, on the other hand, they could not or would not prove to the interrogating officer that they were captured Allied soldiers, their stay in solitary confinement would be indefinite. With that note, he shouted a command and instantly five German armed guards marched into the room, each taking a POW by the elbow, marching them out of the room and onto a landing at the top of a long stairway. The stairway led down into the basement of the building.

Just before descending the stairway to the basement, the POW's were escorted past a small room where a clerk was seated at a metal imprinting machine. As each POW reached his table, he matched the prisoner's paperwork with the prisoner and typed a "dog" tag for each of them. He then secured the metal tag with a nylon chain, handed it to each of the POW's, and instructed them to wear it around his neck. Lovoi looked at his "dog" tag when he received it and noted that his identification number was 8910. He looped the ID chain around his neck and stood by for further instructions.

The next move was to descend the stairway. At the bottom of the stairway, Lovoi and his comrades were escorted into a small latrine where they were given the opportunity to relieve themselves. From the latrine they were escorted down a long dark corridor. On either side of the corridor, and offset from each other, were medium-sized doors. The doors were made of heavy wood and had no windows. Lovoi did notice that the doors had a metal entry panel located several inches off the floor. This panel was about twelve inches wide and six inches high. The metal cover could be locked from the outside. Later, he learned that it was through this panel that his daily meal would be thrust for his consumption. He could not help but compare this scene with those in some movies he'd seen back home, which included such dungeonlike cells. Of course he had never been in solitary confinement before. The introduction to this special kind of torture would further test his courage and resolve. He was determined to endure the consequences without breaking down.

His guard unlocked the cell door, opened it, and shoved Lovoi unceremoniously into its darkness. As quickly as the door was unlocked and opened, it was closed and locked. Lovoi just stood still for a few moments, blinking his eyes and trying to adjust to the darkness. There was a small, fixed, translucent window high on the wall opposite the door. Streaks of light were getting through to give the cell an eerie perception of shadows.

Through the light streaks, he spotted several metal bars protecting the window. The room was unbearably hot and humid. The air within it was heavy and stale. Lovoi took off his thin blanket and jacket. He looked around as if to locate a place to hang them on. He found no such hanger as he examined each of the four walls. In one of the corners of the floor, he found a pile of straw. He surmised that this straw was to be his bed. With nothing but time on his hands, he began a thorough inch-by-inch examination of the cell. The walls consisted of cement blocks, the floor was made of smooth cement, and the ceiling looked as though it was also finished cement. The ceiling was higher than Lovoi could reach, perhaps eight feet. By stepping off the distances along the walls, he guessed that the cell was about five feet wide by eight feet long. The basement was very quiet. There were no sounds to be heard. He wondered if this room was to be his grave. As he began to contemplate his latest dilemma, he felt his body starting to itch.

Unconsciously he gently scratched those areas of his body that were itchy. At first, he thought the itching was due to the heat and humidity of his new environment. But the worst was yet to come. It did not take long for him to realize that the cell was infested with lice and fleas. Were they waiting to greet him on his bed of straw?

Yes, there was no doubt these tiny biting devils were living in the pile of straw that was on the floor in one corner of the cell. He rubbed the exposed part of his body to try to shed the pests. He moved over to the corner diagonally opposite the pile of straw. It was the farthest he could go. He looked around for some relief. But of course there was none to be found. He just began to scratch and scratch and scratch. Good Lord, now they were in his hair. He put his shoulders against the two adjacent walls opposite the flea pile and sagged to a sitting position. He began to perspire. He closed his eyes and prayed. He was very tired, but he dared not sleep. He just kept scratching.

When he awoke he was freezing. It was pitch black in the cell. He looked up at the window, no light came through. He reasoned that the time must be between late evening and early morning. He was losing track of time. He looked for his jacket, blanket, and hat that he had carefully laid on the floor. He put them back on his body to stop the uncontrollable shaking. He was not scratching as much now. Maybe the pests were not as active in cold weather as they were in hot weather.

Solitary

Lovoi thought he might panic at some stage of this confinement. For the first time he felt a combination of anxiety and depression. He fought it off. He tried to count the days since his capture. He guessed five days. He told himself that many other brave young men faced far worse conditions and dangers than he was in and they didn't panic. He told himself that he must get through his first night with resistance and resolve. He recalled the explosion on his B-17 over the Innsbruck target and how fortunate he was to be alive. He felt the hand of God.

The next few hours dragged on unmercifully. Lovoi kept looking up at the small window, searching for the first ray of light announcing the arrival of early dawn. He alternated between pacing the floor and sitting on the hard surface in the corner. His body needed some rest and change from its contact with the cement floor and walls. Finally, he gave in and sat on the pile of straw. He felt weary. He put his arm under his head, lay on his side, and scratched himself to sleep.

When he awoke this time, the cell was bathed in a dim light, thanks to the small window. Lovoi stood up and stretched. He noticed that the walls of the cell had haphazard scratch marks all over them. He was curious and drew closer to examine the marks in detail. Most of them showed a pattern of four vertical scratches and one diagonal scratch that cut across all four of the vertical ones. It did not take long for him to figure out that each of these patterns represented five days, four days by the four vertical lines and one day for the diagonal line. It appeared that each cement block had its own individual identification over the patterns consisting of three initials scratched in the same manner. Nearly every cement block was taken. Lovoi reasoned that the taller previous prisoners used the higher cement blocks and the shorter ones used the middle and lower blocks.

Lovoi looked for an unused block so he could chronicle his solitary time along with those of his comrades. The best he could find was a cement block on the wall opposite the door. He removed his "dog tag" from his neck and began to scratch his initials JWL, at the top of the block he selected. He took his time because he had plenty of it and because he wanted to do a good job. When he completed the "J" of his first name, Joseph, he stood back to examine and admire his work. "Not bad," he mumbled. He continued his artistic labor with the "W" for his middle name, William, and finished it with the "L" for Lovoi. He stepped back again and was heard to say, "Could be straighter, but not bad." Then he carefully drew two parallel vertical lines to record his first two days in this God-forsaken room, whose temperature vacillated between freezing and stifling hot, and whose only other tenants were millions of lice and fleas.

He calculated that by now it must be mid-morning. The room grew brighter, and he was very hungry. He wished he had something to do. He put his ear to the wooden door and listened intently. He heard nothing. He examined the cement block walls again. He carefully counted the number of lines on the blocks to determine what the longest stay was and what the shortest stay was. This data might give him a clue as to how long he would be staying. He found that most of the intervals ran between five and ten days. But he did locate one block with a twelve-day stay imprinted under the initials "GBS."

His searching was interrupted by the sound of booted footsteps approaching along the corridor. Every minute or two, the sounds vanished and then were heard again.

With each stop, the sounds grew louder. Now he could hear the squeaking of wheels slowly turning as well. And then the footsteps and wheels stopped outside of his door. The small entry panel at the bottom of the door opened. Lovoi watched as a large bowl of food was inserted by the person in the corridor. A loud muffled voice gave some instruction that Lovoi did not recognize, but he surmised it to mean that he should reach down and receive the offering before it spilled.

He quickly bent down and received the bowl in both hands. It was warm and had a spoon handle sticking out of its contents. It smelled good. Lovoi decided to eat this meal in a standing position so he didn't have to share it with his tiny cell mates. It was a cabbage soup, rather thick, and laced with several large pieces of turnip slices. There was no meat in the meal, but it tasted very hearty. Lovoi wasted no time in consuming it. He felt satisfied for the time being. After he licked the bowl and spoon clean, he pushed them through the small panel at the bottom of the door. He thought that was the best thing to do with the dirty dish and spoon. Besides, he did not want to give his pesky friends another reason to hang around.

About an hour later, the booted footsteps were heard coming down the corridor again. Lovoi's heart jumped as he realized that they had stopped outside his door. He heard a key turn the lock, and then the door was shoved open. The lighted corridor shed some of its energy into the open cell and gave Lovoi cause to hesitate and rub his eyes. Two German guards were standing in the doorway. They wore side arms. One of them waved Lovoi out of the cell and into the corridor. One guard stepped in front of him while the other guard brought up the rear of the three-man single file procession. It marched down the corridor toward the stairway, which led up to the interrogation room. On the way, the guards stopped by the latrine and offered Lovoi a chance to use the facility. He did. The walk then continued up the stairs and to the closed door of the interrogation room. Here the lead guard rapped his fist on the door panel. The door opened promptly revealing a large room, well lighted by a number of wall light fixtures. The floor appeared to be decorated with marble tile covered for the most part with a dark red oriental rug, which ran the length of the entry way to a large mahogany desk at the farthest end.

As Lovoi marched into the room, he noted out of the corners of his eyes that there were several German officers and noncoms sitting at a few cluttered desks and tables located on both side walls. The end of the room with the mahogany desk was framed by several floor-to-ceiling windows that allowed natural light into the room as well as providing an interesting view of the winter landscape of snow-covered trees and bushes posing in white and green juxtaposition. The leather swivel chair that belonged to the desk was occupied by a German officer, who introduced himself as a colonel. On the opposite side of the large desk was a wooden armchair. Lovoi was motioned to sit there.

The Colonel began the conversation with an explanation of the necessity to determine positively the identification of the prisoners who were captured as a result of military action. He stressed this necessity because the treatment accorded to prisoners was quite different than the treatment accorded to spies. In the first case, the warring parties followed the general rules of the Geneva Convention. In the second case, that of spies, death was the usual punishment for such unfortunate captives. And so the interrogation began.

The Colonel asked, "Name?" Lovoi answered "Joseph W. Lovoi." "What is your rank?" Lovoi answered "Second Lieutenant." (He had not learned of his promotion to First Lieutenant yet.) The promotion was granted on November 9, 1944, and this day was November 21, 1944. "And your serial number?" the Colonel continued. "0-718364" came the answer. So far, so good. The Colonel spoke perfect English. He comported himself with dignity and respect. He was spotlessly dressed in a crisp uniform and bore good posture.

From here on the interrogation gradually deteriorated to the level of unanswered questions. "What is the location of your base? Who is your commanding officer? What type aircraft were you flying? What was your position in the crew? How many missions have you flown?" were all questions that Lovoi would not give answers to, citing the rules of the Geneva Convention, restricting the prisoner to give only his name, rank, and serial number. Lovoi could see that under the veil of cool calmness exhibited by the Colonel, he was becoming exasperated with the non-answers that Lovoi was giving him.

And so the first attempt at interrogation came to an abrupt end. The Colonel turned his back on Lovoi and ordered him to be removed from the room. In less time than it takes to tell it, Lovoi was out of the room, down the stairs, through the corridor, and back in his cell. For a moment Lovoi just stood there. He was not sure if his first encounter with the Colonel was a success or a failure. Time would tell. He was hopeful because he was still alive.

It was another twenty-four hours or so before the scene just played out was repeated. In the meantime, Lovoi had scratched another vertical line on "his" cement block, had another bowl of soup, had fought back the pangs of anxiety and depression, had felt the humid heat of the day and the dry cold of the night, and scratched away at most of the exposed parts of his body. He recalled with some bitterness that none of this period of captivity was ever discussed in his training classes at the Selman Field Navigation School in Monroe, Louisiana. He thought his role as a World War II military officer was to preserve the freedom that his forefathers had won about one hundred fifty years ago, and to use that freedom as a catalyst to chase his very own American Dream. His black-and-white world was starting to show some dark traces as he realized that this phase of his military tour, that of a prisoner at the mercy of his enemy, was a part of the price he was to pay for the privilege of chasing his American Dream!

Lovoi's second meeting with the Colonel lasted a little longer. Between some of the unanswered questions, they discussed the Brooklyn Dodgers and the New York Yankees. It unnerved Lovoi a little to realize that this German officer was in possession of American lore and language while he himself knew very little about Germany and its social pastimes. Nevertheless, he believed that he was acting in a correct military way by standing by his vow to give only his name, rank, and serial number. He shuddered to think of what fate might await him. Again he was summarily dismissed back to his dismal dank cell, but this time he had reason to worry. The Colonel showed visible signs of impatience.

That night the translucent window at the top of his cell wall seemed to allow more light to be transmitted than usual. He could see the interior of the cell more clearly. He even thought he could see the fleas hopping on and off his person. Suddenly, he heard an air-raid siren wailing somewhere in the distance. It was an irritating sound and continued for some time, perhaps thirty minutes. And then the wail was drowned out by the crashing series of explosions. The earth shuddered, creating tremors that reminded Lovoi this was his first experience on the receiving of an air raid. The earth shook again and again for the better part of thirty minutes. Lovoi prayed that the building he was in was not a target. Then there followed a wakelike silence for a short moment. The "all clear" siren next screamed its message that the Allied air raid was over. Minutes later the sound of fire engine trucks and raucous horns could be faintly heard in the distance. Lovoi was grateful that he had dodged another bullet.

He was surprised to find that he would not be interrogated the next day. As usual he scratched another vertical line, the fourth, on "his" cement block. By now he was really in need of a bath, a shave, clean clothes, and even a haircut. Although, grooming had a low position on his priority list, which was headed by SURVIVAL, it was still on the list. It was during this day of inactivity that he recalled one of his training missions. It had been a night flight from Shreveport, Louisiana, to Amarillo, Texas. The training aircraft was a C-60 twin-engine trainer. The crew complement of eight airmen included two pilots, a navigation instructor, and five young navigation cadets. This was a night mission. There were six aircraft involved. The flight to Amarillo was without incident. The training session was accomplished and after the group of six aircraft landed, the entire crews headed for the mess hall at the Amarillo Air Base for dinner. Late that evening, having finished the meal, all forty-eight airmen headed for the flight line to prepare for the training flight back to Shreveport.

During the preflight procedure of the C-60 trainers, one of the aircraft proved to have a faulty engine. It was decided to RON (Remain Over Night) the two pilots and the navigation instructor until the next day so they could supervise the repair of the faulty engine and fly the trainer back to Shreveport. The five students of the disabled aircraft were instructed to spread themselves, one in each of the remaining aircraft so they could complete the round-trip night mission. Three of the five students ran to the three nearest aircraft. The last two students, one of whom was Lovoi, had to run to the ramp to board the two remaining trainers waiting to take off.

Lovoi deferred to his comrade to choose which aircraft he wanted to fly in. Then he ran to the last available trainer and boarded it. Subsequently, the first three aircraft took off and began the flight to Shreveport. The fourth aircraft to take off was the one that Lovoi's classmate chose. From his position in the navigator's seat in the fifth aircraft, which was about to taxi toward the runway for its takeoff, Lovoi watched as the fourth aircraft began its takeoff roll and pick up speed to clear the runaway. Its takeoff seemed to be quite normal, and by the time it reached the end of the runway, it must have been above five hundred feet.

And then it happened. The aircraft was pulling its wheels up when there was a brilliant flash of light followed by a loud explosion and a red fireball. The plane carrying his buddy had exploded and its burning wreckage was hurtling earthward carrying all nine passengers to an early grave. Lovoi had dodged a bullet. He believed that he resurrected this particular memory from the deep recesses of his mind because the word SURVIVAL began to haunt him. He started to associate each bullet that he had dodged with that word. And this training incident vividly flashed before him at this time and in this cell.

It was on the fifth day of solitary that the stand-off between the Colonel and the Lieutenant was broken. After he devoured his bowl of warm soup, he was escorted into the now familiar interrogation room. This time the Colonel tried a different approach. He actually surprised Lovoi with his knowledge of Lovoi's childhood, education, family history, exact address, and military training locations. He rattled off the names of his parents and several of his siblings, and where his family lived. He identified his high school as Cambridge Latin. He smugly recalled Lovoi's graduation from navigation school at Monroe, Louisiana. The Colonel paused and stared out the window for effect.

A moment later, he faced Lovoi, folded his arms, and stared into his eyes. Again he paused giving the surprise element a chance to sink in. Then he asked in a moderate, level tone, "Do you think that this information is accurate?" Lovoi nodded his head and said, "Not bad, Colonel." "Well," said the Colonel, "your intelligence is even better than ours." Then Lovoi offered, "If you knew all these things, wasn't it clear to you that I am a legitimate prisoner of war?" "Yes," he answered, "but we have to be sure that you were indeed Joseph W. Lovoi." Then he cocked his head and wryly smiled. "For you the war is over."

VI

Shipped into Cold Storage

As Lovoi was being led back to his cell for perhaps the last time, he mused to himself, "Yes, the hot war may be over, but the war of survival has just begun." When he was well inside of his cell, he drew the fifth and diagonal line across the four vertical ones on "his" cement block. He felt pride that he has passed this test of loyalty to his country. He felt exhausted now that the ordeal seemed to be over. He sat back against the cell wall and tasted his warm tears as he lost control of his emotional rigidity.

He spent the remainder of the fifth day in anticipation of what the next event might be. He wondered if he was really in the clear from the interrogation center and if so, when and where he would be sent to serve his time until the war was over.

That night he sat on his bed of straw and pulled his knees up to his chin. He rested his grimy face on his folded arms and buried his head. He began to tremble. The emotional letdown was taking its toll. He held one arm out straight and watched it tremble uncontrollably. He knew something was happening to him and it scared him. He tried to talk to himself and reassure himself of his sanity. He closed his eyes and wished himself back to Foggia, Italy. There he was free and useful.

One of the most memorable moments of his life occurred to him in Foggia. There he had met Lucia. He

Lucia

met her at the Red Cross Club where lucky airmen who returned alive from their bombing missions came to relax and have coffee with sandwiches. She was a young and beautiful nineteen-year-old Italian girl, with a husky voice and friendly smile. Her father was killed in an Allied air raid. She, her brother Nino, and her mother lived in a second-floor apartment of a bombed-out apartment house. She loved to talk with Lovoi because his Italian speech was so bad that it was the subject of friendly banter.

The other officers at the club envied him because he seemed to have the "inside track" with Lucia. But what they did not know was that true to Italian tradition, the Lieutenant and Lucia were never alone together. Either her brother, her mother, or both were within eyesight at all times. However, they did manage to stir warm adolescent feelings within each other in spite of their limited privacy.

Lucia loved American music and often hummed some of the more popular songs. Lovoi taught her the words to several of them, one in particular, "You Are Always in My Heart." The incident that crossed Lovoi's mind as he sat on the straw pile scratching himself occurred on a Saturday evening in early November, 1944. The Red Cross Club had closed at midnight. Lovoi offered to drive Lucia and her mother the short distance back to her apartment in his jeep. The offer was accepted, and off they went, carefully picking their way through the bomb-cratered streets and dark alleyways.

On the way home, Lucia's mother, who was sitting in the back seat, dozed off. Lovoi reached his right hand over to Lucia's left hand and clasped it firmly. He stared straight ahead. This was the first time they had any bodily contact. She returned the grip and laid her head on the back of her seat, closed her eyes, and softly sang, "You Are Always in My Heart, Even Though You're Far Away." She hummed the rest of it and returned Lovoi's hand squeezes, one for one. When they arrived at the apartment, Lucia's mother had awakened. The three of them exited the jeep, and climbed the two stories to the four-room apartment. When they reached the kitchen, Lucia's mother excused herself and left to take off her coat in her bedroom. Lucia and Lovoi looked at each other and in a flash, they embraced and magnetically locked themselves. Not a word was said. None was needed. He gently brushed his lips against her cheek and tasted her loveliness. A moment later they were apart just in the nick of time. Her mother had returned to the kitchen. Lovoi could hardly contain his happiness. He felt the awakening of a sensation he had never experienced in all his 22 years. He turned to her mother and said, "Bona Serra, Signora," and then to Lucia, "Bona Serra, Lucia." They exchanged a knowing glance and he was gone. He bounded down the stairs and into the jeep. He knew then that he was in love with her. But that was the last time he saw her.

On the morning of the sixth day of his solitary confinement, the usual footsteps stopped outside his door. But this time there was no bowl of soup with a spoon sticking out of it. This time the door was thrown all the way open. The Lieutenant looked up at the guards with a questioning expression on his face. The guards indicated to him that he was to take his blanket and outer clothing and come with them. Lovoi, though thankful for this change of routine, became apprehensive again.

The guards led him to the latrine at the end of the corridor and handed him a small paper bag. He looked inside the bag and saw soap, toothbrush, toothpaste, shaving cream, a comb, and a safety razor. One of the guards indicated that he was to disrobe and exchange his soiled underwear for a clean set, and his outer clothing was gathered for a thorough delousing. As the guard with the soiled clothing left the scene, he tossed Lovoi a towel. The second guard remained to keep tabs on him.

Lovoi was ecstatic. He relished every phase of the grooming ritual. For the first time, he was able to see the many flea and lice bites all over his body. It felt refreshing to use a toothbrush again. He gave himself a very clean shave, not knowing when he might have the opportunity again. His hair was not too long and after he parted it and combed it, he stared at his image in the small mirror over the sink. He was satisfied that on a scale of ten, his physical appearance rated about five. The wound he suffered, when the Italian soldier had hit him on the neck with his rifle, had scabbed over and did not appear to be infected.

Lovoi waited in the latrine with just the clean set of underwear on. He and the guard made small talk with hand signs. After thirty minutes or so, the other guard appeared with an armful of deloused clothing and tossed them over to Lovoi. He put on his old clothes, and they were still warm from the delousing oven. Then he was marched up the stairs and into the entry hall of the interrogation building. Here he joined several other Allied prisoners whose war was over also.

There were several buses parked just outside of the building waiting to be loaded with prisoners who had been cleared. They were to be incarcerated in various German prisoner of war camps. The Allied prisoners who had the rank of officers were assigned to one type of prison compound called Stalag Luft while the noncommissioned officers and airmen were assigned to Stalags.

As soon as a bus load of prisoners accumulated in the foyer of the building, they were identified, loaded on one of the waiting buses, and transported to the distribution center at Wetzlar.

The group that Lovoi was with were mostly Americans. It seemed that they could not stop talking, they had so much to say. It was a psychological relief to see and communicate with friends after the physical and mental stress of the events of the last ten days. Many of the prisoners suffered similar episodes of being shot out of the skies, captured, interrogated, and assigned to a POW camp. It was a very short bus ride to the distribution center. The prisoners were carefully counted and identified by "dog tag" numbers and marched into the building.

The building itself looked to be an abandoned assembly factory with large empty rooms. The POW's were herded into one of these rooms until it was nearly filled. There must have been over 100 of them. It was now noontime and everyone was very hungry. The excitement of what was happening was bittersweet. It meant the end of solitary and interrogation, but it meant the beginning of a phase of incarceration, fear, vulnerability, and the unknown.

During the excitement caused by the limited freedom, i.e., the reunion of some of the prisoners with one another and the sounds of the English language being spoken, the arrival of a German officer with his staff and an American Red Cross representative went unnoticed for the most part.

As the word got around that the German staff was about to address the crowd of prisoners, a gradual hush settled among them and gave way to dead silence. The German officer, a major, stepped up to a dais, scanned the room, and waited for the silence to peak.

And then, in perfect English, the major reiterated what the German colonel had stated back at the interrogation center, i.e., having established that the prisoners were found to be genuine prisoners of war, they had been assigned to various prison camps throughout Germany for the duration of hostilities. He particularly stressed that as prisoners they were to obey the rules of the prison camps and their operative command. He emphasized and underscored the statement that any attempt or attempts at escape would be dealt with severely. Punishment for such a "crime" could be as severe as death. When he had finished what he wished to say, he turned the assembly over to an International Red Cross representative.

The Red Cross representative went on to explain that the German term for "prisoner of war" was *Kriegsgefangen*. This term was thankfully shortened to Kriegie. Therefore, all Allied POW's were referred to as Kriegies. He also encouraged the Kriegies to seek out and find friends and comrades within the group in order to ease the tensions and fears that the Kriegies were experiencing. He reminded the POW's that they were to follow all military procedures that the German Luft commanders required them to observe.

The prison camps were organized in such a way that the highest rated Allied officer in the camp was in charge of the Kriegies' welfare. He interfaced with the German camp commandant in all matters that concerned the operation of the camp. He finished by stating that every camp was operated slightly differently from every other in some respects, but the basic rules of discipline and escape penalties were standard. Finally he announced that each Kriegie would be given a box lunch and a wooden carrying case filled with bare necessities. The lunch was compliments of the International Red Cross, and the wooden case and its contents, compliments of the American YMCA.

During the time it took to organize the distribution of the lunches and wooden boxes, Lovoi looked around the crowded room for a familiar face. He saw none. Some of the other Kriegies were more fortunate. Cries of joy were heard throughout the room as some of the comrades were reunited. There was a lot of back slapping and hand shaking. Yes, and even some hugging.

Lovoi scanned the room as best he could. For a moment he thought he saw a familiar face, but it proved to be that of another single Kriegie looking for the same thing. Their glances crossed, passed each other, and returned. Lovoi and this fellow Kriegie looked at each other, shrugged their shoulders, and proceeded to approach. They shook hands and introduced themselves. Lovoi's friend was a young, boyish-looking Second Lieutenant from the Ninth Air Force. His name was Onofrio Brancato, who hailed from Cuyahoga Falls, Ohio, just a few miles from Akron. The two lieutenants hit it off almost immediately. The chemistry must have been right. It did not take long for them to realize that they were the same age, had similar ambitions of higher educational goals, came from Italian immigrant parents, and had multiple siblings. They had the same approximate physical build and height.

They exchanged their military tour data, and here the similarities drastically divided. Lovoi was stationed in Italy with the Fifteenth Air Force, flew 29 bombing missions in a heavy B-17 bomber, and was a radar navigator. His Kriegie friend was stationed with the Ninth Air Force in France, flew 3 bombing missions in a medium B-26 bomber, and was a co-pilot. These differences in military background gave them lots of fodder for many conversations to come as their friendship grew and solidified.

The box lunches and the wooden cases were distributed. The hungry Kriegies went through the box lunches in record time. It had been awhile since they tasted tuna fish sandwiches, hard apples, cookies, chocolate, chewing gum, and cigarettes. Had they even suspected that this was to be their last full meal for months to come, they might have taken the time to savor it.

The wooden cases from the YMCA contained more lasting gifts. These included underwear, woolen gloves, woolen cap, army shirt, army pants, toiletry, chewing gum, cigarettes, playing cards, socks, needle and thread, candy, sugar, and jam.

At last the time for the trip to the railroad station was at hand. Several army-type busses were parked outside the distribution center waiting for their passengers. The Kriegies were lined up in rows of threes and identified by "dog tag" number. Then they were marched out of the assembly room, into the corridor, and to the foyer of the center. The change in temperature was startling. It was very cold in the foyer. The Kriegies pulled their newly acquired woolen hats tightly over their heads, pulled on their woolen gloves, and tightened their coat collars around their necks.

The German winter was upon them. It was a clear day, late in the afternoon, what was left of the sunshine was leaving fast. When the Kriegies exited the distribution center to board the busses, they bent their heads to parry the cold bite of the frigid air. The bus that Lovoi and Brancato were assigned to was heatless. The seats were cold and the windows were frosted. When the two new friends spoke to each other, they could see each other's breath as it quickly vaporized.

Well, the two lieutenants could not go around much longer calling each other Lovoi and Brancato. It took too much energy. So they decided to call each other by their shortened names or nicknames. Lovoi's was relatively easy, "Joe." On the other hand, Brancato's was an improvement, "Nuffrie." And so it was that Joe and Nuffrie were to create a friendship, born of identical needy circumstances and raised with honor, dignity, and true loyalty.

The bus ride to the railroad station was a short one. The intensity of the cold weather was better tolerated since the Kriegies had their bellies full and clean clothing to wear. It was somewhat comical to see that they were all chewing gum and gabbing at the same time. Yes, even the guards were chewing gum.

As they boarded a special section of the train, the Kriegies were counted again. The Kriegie count had to be exact or no one moved. This was just the beginning of the *appel* (roll call) phase of their incarceration. Practically, the only way that the German command could keep track of their human prizes was to keep track of their numbers.

The train also carried civilians and German military personnel in its passenger sections. The rear railroad cars were loaded with freight. It was a long train that finally began its journey to its various stops. The hour was late. The Kriegie section of the train became quiet as its passengers rested their heads on the back rests of the cold wooden seats. Some of them were asleep, thank God. Some of them were having a hard time coming to grips with the reality of their situation. In the waning dimness of the night, Lovoi could see some of the faces of his comrades. Suddenly, they did not look like young twenty-one-year-olds any more. Then, he too fell asleep.

At some point during the night, the train jolted to a stop, waking up nearly all of its passengers. Lovoi looked out the window for any sign of civilization. He saw none. The train appeared to be stopped alongside the edge of a wooded area. And then, about fifteen minutes later, the wail of a distant air-raid alarm could be heard. The Allied bombers were at it again. It was a clear night and the targets lacked the protection of cloud cover. Luckily, the target for this night was far enough from the train's location that none of the fire bombs came near it. Minutes later the distant sky began to glow, attesting to the grisly effect of the night bombing mission. The Kriegies were silent. Some of them were happy to witness the success of this bombing mission. Some of them were sad to witness the cruel devastation of humanity and civilization. And some of them had no feelings, the barbaric consequences of what was going on were incomprehensible to their young black-and-white-shaded minds.

The train lay in hiding for the next few hours. Then its engine blasted its intention to continue its journey and slowly picked up speed and momentum. The rest of the night was uneventful, except for several stops to let passengers off and on. Lovoi tried to catch a glimpse of the identification signs along the station platforms. He could not make out any of the signs. It was too dark to see clearly.

As the pinkish dawn broke in the east, he concluded that the train was heading in a general northeast direction. When several hours later he did recognize the sign of the station that they were stopped at, as Leipzig, his fears were verified. The train was traveling northeast toward Berlin and away from the battle lines. He felt as though he were being buried deeper and deeper into the frozen bowels of a vengeful enemy.

The train continued its journey all that day. Apart from its frequent stops, it continued to put distance between its passenger load of Kriegies and the Allied front lines. The cloudy weather was conducive to travel since the Allied bombers and low-level strafing aircraft could not operate in such weather. It was now nearly twenty-four hours since the Kriegies had been herded aboard this train. With each stop the civilian passenger count diminished, leading Lovoi to assume that the train was nearing its destination where it would deliver its load of Kriegie passengers to their prison compound. And so it was.

Late in the afternoon amid a swirling snowstorm carried in on the wings of a frigid cold front, the train stopped for its last time. The only passengers left on it were the Allied POW's. There were several busses waiting at the station to pick up and deliver the Kriegies to Stalag Luft III. The train stopped at a small town called Sagan, just about a hundred miles east by southeast of Berlin. It was nestled just inside Germany's Polish border. The bus ride from the depot to the prison compound was a short one, and it was accomplished in the face of a blinding blizzard.

The Kriegies were counted when they were loaded on the busses, and they were again counted when they were off-loaded at the barbed-wire gates of the prison compound. The men were lined up in formation, five across and ten deep. They stood at attention on command while the horizontal blast of snowflakes melted on their faces. The scene was awesome. Huge klieg lights, two each on top of two light poles on both sides of the barbed-wire gate, shot their energy past the falling snow and entrapped the new arrivals in its glaring clutches.

Kriegies arrive at Stalag Luft III

The Kriegies were nearly blinded by the combination of high-intensity lights and blowing cold snowflakes that settled on their faces. It seemed to take forever for the compound personnel vehicles to reach the group of frozen Kriegies. They were ordered to load quickly onto the busses and find a seat. As each bus was filled with the appropriate number of POW's and guards, it moved through the Stalag gate and into the compound grounds. Each bus then stopped outside a small guard house where its driver received final delivery instructions.

The Stalag Luft III was divided into five camps, North, South, East, West, and Center. The arriving POW's were being delivered to existing vacancies within these camps. Lovoi and Brancato managed to stay together throughout all these maneuvers and ended up being delivered to the North Camp. The North Camp was occupied mostly by officers from England, Canada, Scotland, and Australia. And so it was, on that late November afternoon in the face of a blinding snowstorm that Lieutenants Lovoi and Brancato were introduced to their new permanent quarters and to their English-speaking roommates with the funny accents.

VII

Getting to Know the Brits

The compound bus made its way slowly in the snowstorm from one camp to the other, dropping off Kriegies as they were assigned. Lovoi and Brancato were the last two passengers to be let off the bus. They were delivered to the North Camp where they were received very warmly. The Kriegies in the barracks to which they were assigned made them feel welcome. Of course the welcome had two emotional levels, a high because the newcomers were safe and sound, and a low because they were unfortunate to be captured and face the hardships that confronted them.

The room to which the two Americans were assigned already had sixteen other Kriegies in it, and they were all air crew members of the Royal Air Force (RAF), the Royal Canadian Air Force (RCAF), and the Royal Australian Air Force (RAAF). The two Americans arrived at the dinner hour as the food was being prepared for the sixteen Kriegies. Joe and Nuffrie were invited to join the group, but they had to agree that they would pool their future Red Cross food parcels and their shares of the German food contributions with the rest of the roommates.

The living quarters consisted basically of a large room approximately 20 by 20 feet. It was not only their living quarters but their sleeping quarters. There were six triple bunk beds, which accommodated the eighteen Kriegies. Each barracks included five such rooms and a cooking area with a stove. The stove was assigned to be used by each room for dinner preparation purposes on a rotating basis. For example, Room #1 would use the stove from 5:00 to 5:30 P.M. Room #2 would use it from 5:30 to 6:00 P.M. Room #3 would use it from 6:00 to 6:30 P.M. Room #4 would use it from 6:30 to 7:00 P.M., and Room #5 would use it from 7:00 to 7:30 P.M.

This arrangement would rotate each week so that each of the five rooms experienced the same inconvenience of a shifting dinner hour. Another reason for the shifting arrangement, and perhaps the more important one, was that the room assigned to use the stove first would have to use more fuel to bring the stove up to cooking temperature. Fuel was a very precious necessity.

The winter was an unusually cold one. The German command was very stingy with the fuel allotments. The fuel was made from pressed coal dust briquettes. Each room was allocated a certain number of these briquettes. They had to use them wisely or they might run out of fuel before their next allotment. This would mean cold meals until the allotment was refilled. Obviously, the room that used the stove last had a huge advantage. By the time it was their turn to use the stove, it was almost red hot. So the number of briquettes needed to cook their meal was minimal.

On the day Joe Lovoi arrived at Stalag Luft III, he was under the weather. He had a bad cold and some trouble breathing. He was happy to be assigned a bunk, a lower one, so he could lie down and pull his blanket tightly around him. When time came for dinner, he felt miserable and sick. The dinner meal was a slice of black bread with a tuna fish spread accompanied with a cup of barley soup sweetened with raisins. When it was time to be seated and "dig in," Joe begged off, pleading nausea. A dead silence greeted his plea. No one in the history of Stalag Luft III had ever passed up a meal. It was unheard of. As a matter of fact, food was so scarce that such a move was tantamount to insanity.

Of course Lovoi did not realize that just within the next few days, he too would be feeling the gnawing pangs of hunger and rue the day when he passed up a meal. It was decided to draw straws for Joe's meal. It was divided among the four longest straws.

Getting to know the British was an interesting adventure. Their reputations had preceded them in America via the movies, the inter-country travel between the United States and Canada, between the United States and Europe, and to a lesser extent, between the United States and Australia. These British airmen seemed to be more mature than their American counterparts. They certainly knew a lot more about what was going on in this European war and its history than did the American Kriegies.

Lovoi was able to observe slight differences among his English, Canadian, and Australian roommates. The English were more gregarious, the Canadians looked and acted more like Americans, and the Australians seemed more reserved. Lovoi admired the spirit and bravery of each of these British flyers, but he especially respected the courage of the English members of the RAF. Invariably, when a rule-breaking camp situation arose that needed to be mediated with the German staff, it was the English ranking officer who negotiated the ultimate ruling. He seemed to command more respect from the German Staff. For this reason, Lovoi was happy to be in their company. And the German guards were more compliant to the English arguments than to the American positions. It didn't surprise Lovoi to notice the subtle differences. After all, the English and the Germans were geographically located only a channel apart.

The days dragged on. Lovoi learned how to play bridge and chess. The British were good at these games. But the nights were depressing. Each night the eighteen young men bundled up in their clothes and blankets, closed their eyes and tried to find that elusive sedative, sleep. In the privacy of the darkness, Lovoi allowed his thoughts to wander without restraint or direction, peeling his memory as the mood required. He remembered a particular solo mission that called for a single bomber to deliver bombs on the oil refineries just outside the city of Vienna, Austria.

When the weather was bad, socked in, too cloudy to field a formation of B-17's because the visibility between aircraft was below minimums, the group commander of the 463rd Bomb Group in Foggia, Italy, would order certain targets to be hit by single B-17's. The mission took advantage of the cloudy weather by deliberately flying a course to the target that was fraught with clouds, the thicker, the better. The bomber would "hide" in the cloud layers so that it could not be detected by the Luftwaffe's interceptors.

And as the B-17 approached the Initial Point of the bomb run, the waist gunners would toss out bundles of chaff, shredded aluminum material. The chaff created a diversionary target to confuse the anti-aircraft gunners, sometimes giving the bomber a flakless path to the target. Well, at least that was the theory. The total mission was under the control of the radar navigator, for it was he who gave the pilot the headings to the IP and target. He was able to "see" the terrain with his airborne radar.

Lovoi recalled on this particular mission an incident that was life threatening, but had a happy ending. When the B-17 reached the altitude of ten-thousand feet, it was a practice to touch base with each of the crew members at every one-thousand feet of increased altitude. Each crew member was roll-called to be sure that his oxygen system was working. Everything went well until the roll call at eighteen-thousand feet was made through the intercommunication system. Each crew member answered the roll except the left waist gunner. The bombardier asked the right waist gunner if the left waist gunner was okay. The right waist gunner reported that the left waist gunner was lying motionless on the floor of the aircraft. The bombardier asked Lovoi to go back and investigate.

Lovoi immediately switched his oxygen supply hose from the main system to a mobile "walk around" oxygen bottle. He rushed into the main fuselage and bent down to see what the problem was. The left waist gunner was lying motionless. He removed the waist gunner's oxygen mask and then his own mask. He placed his mask on the waist gunner's face while he held his breath. He then took his mask off the waist gunner's face and took a few sucks of oxygen himself. He quickly replaced his mask on the waist gunner's face. This time the waist gunner moved a little. His eyes fluttered.

Lovoi repeated the mask switching once more because he was getting a little dizzy himself. By now both Lovoi and the waist gunner were sharing Lovoi's oxygen mask. Then Lovoi stuck his index finger in the breathing valve of the waist gunner's mask and scooped out a large piece of ice. Apparently, the butterfly valve in the waist gunner's mask had jammed with the waist gunner's frozen expiration. Now Lovoi put the waist gunner's mask back on the waist gunner's face, and his own mask on himself. Both airmen were now out of danger. When Lovoi was certain that the waist gunner was okay, he called in to the bombardier and told him that the waist gunner was the victim of a "bad ice cube." As he turned to go back to his position, the waist gunner held Lovoi by the shoulders for a moment and gave him a grateful expression.

Lovoi never forgot that look. And this night, for no particular reason, the memory of that moment dallied for a long time in his memory. The night chill had spread over Stalag Luft III. In the dimness of the room, Lovoi could see his vaporized breath. It was cold. No, it was bone chilling cold. Lovoi tried to find some sleep. The silence in the room was broken throughout the night by uncontrollable coughing, throat clearing, and intermittent raling. None of the Kriegies slept peacefully.

And then it was morning. There was a reluctance to get up from the bunk because there was nothing to look forward to, just *appel* (roll call). Just another day of cold, hunger, and waiting. But the daily routine called for the breakfast preparer of the week to rise early and perform the cutting of the bread and the spreading of the jam. This chore was assigned to a different Kriegie on a weekly basis until all eighteen of them rose early to cut the break and spread the jam. Then the cycle was repeated.

The cutting of the bread was a surgical operation. The loaf of black bread had to be cut into eighteen equal slices. This job demanded a keen eye, a steady hand, and a sense of fairness. The two end slices were to be avoided because, of course, they were a bit smaller due to the rounded ends of the loaf of bread. It was usual for the bread cutter to take one of the end pieces, but the other end slice had to be distributed.

On one particular morning, Lovoi ended up with the last slice, the end piece. It happened because the server deliberately passed him up as he made his round of the bunks. When seventeen other slices were taken, the server came back to Lovoi's bunk and offered him the last piece, the end slice. Lovoi was upset, but he said not a word. He just accepted the incident and tucked it away in his memory. Several weeks later, when he was the early rising breakfast preparer, he reached back into his memory of this incident and returned the favor to the Kriegie who had unfairly served him the end slice several weeks ago. That Kriegie's name was James. James said not a word regarding the incident. He knew that the score was being evened. And that incident was never repeated again among the eighteen Kriegies who occupied that room. Food was more precious than gold.

In a room full of eighteen bright, young, and talented men, there usually is one who either likes to cook or has had some experience with the art. In Lovoi's room, there was an Australian Kriegie who had had actual experience as a second cook in an exclusive restaurant in Sydney, Australia. He was unanimously chosen to prepare such meals as the available ingredients would warrant.

Each Kriegie was allotted one American Red Cross food parcel every other week. To get maximum benefit from this allotment, the fish, meat, and chicken cans of food were pooled into one larder. The parcel ingredients were cans of fish, powdered milk, sugar, cans of Spam, margarine, jam, cans of chicken, and paté. The rest of the contents such as cigarettes, candy, chewing gum, and crackers were kept by each Kriegie to consume as he wished. The cook had to prepare 18 meals each day for 14 days, or a total of 252 dinner meals.

The 18 Red Cross food parcels were designed to prepare just 126 meals and had to be supplemented by the German allotment of barley, sauerkraut, and fish cheese. The barley was quite palatable and if cooked to excess, it would almost double in size. The question became, was it worth the trade-off of extra fuel for the extra bulk? The sauerkraut could be eaten if it was fried to get rid of the acidic content, but the fish cheese was almost putrid. Only in the hungriest situation would any of the Kriegies eat the fish cheese. The Germans also allotted two loaves of black bread per day, per room, two slices per Kriegie.

So, the breakfast for each Kriegie consisted of one slice of black bread spread with jam and a cup of tea or ersatz coffee. The lunch was also a slice of black bread, but spread with paté, served with tea or coffee. The breakfast and lunch were eaten in an informal manner. The Kriegies either sat on their bunks, or at the table, or gathered in chatting groups. The dinners were consumed in a more formal manner. All eighteen Kriegies sat at the large kitchen table and were served by the cook. Here, again, the serving operation was handled with the skill of a chemist in a laboratory. The cook had to be careful that each ladle full of food was the same size for all eighteen Kriegies. Each spoonful of barley was equal to all the other spoonsful of barley. And, if after meting out eighteen servings there was any left, this residue had to be divided fairly among eighteen Kriegies. On the rare occasion when the cook misjudged the ladle amounts and ended up with only seventeen servings, the seventeen servings were returned to the pot and the serving process was repeated. This time the cook was careful to have at least eighteen servings to go around. Food was more precious than gold.

Of course, there never was enough food to sustain the Kriegies in a manner that was anywhere near fulfilling. And so they lost weight, became somewhat emaciated, and to save energy acted listlessly. The Kriegies who had been incarcerated for long periods of time, such as over one or two years, looked the worst. Their cheekbones, ribs, and limb joints were quite noticeable. Those Kriegies who had been captured within the last six months were drawn, but they still had enough energy to take daily walks around the compound and even throw a ball, weather permitting.

Time was an enemy. While it did not physically abuse the Kriegie, it did drag over his spirit and bare his mortality. The days passed slowly accompanied by cold temperatures and much snowfall. But the nights were brutal. There weren't enough blankets and covers to keep the chill from penetrating into the bones.

Nuffrie had been a music major before he enlisted in the military service. His specialty was the guitar. He had a very pleasant voice to go along with that instrument as well. It only took about one carton of cigarettes to convince one of the guards to procure a used instrument and slip it past the entry gate and into the barracks. Nuffrie tuned the guitar by ear and began strumming some of the old favorites as the mood directed him. The whole room full of Kriegies would stop their activities and sit close to Nuffrie's bunk and listen. The music seemed to inject new life into them as they swayed back and forth with the music. Some of them even joined Nuffrie vocally. The results were very pleasing. And so it was that nearly every night Nuffrie would strum on his guitar and the rest of the young men gathered around him and showed off their vocal talents or lack thereof. This sing-along reminded the men of home.

The songs that were popular in the United States were the same songs that were popular in Canada, England, and Australia. The accents were a little different but the music was the same. Gradually, even the Kriegies from the other rooms in the barracks visited Nuffrie's corner and joined in on the singing. It was a pleasant sound, the more singers the more joyous the chorus. Sometimes, when a particular song was unknown to the audience, Nuffrie would sing it solo. His soft voice and boyish smile were indeed the essence of the "All American Boy." His performance and personality were magnetic. He became a true idol of the North Camp.

The German winter was beginning to grip the Silesian countryside. The Oder River was frozen solid. The Kriegies were spending more and more time in bed and less time walking and exercising. It was early December and Christmas of 1944 was approaching. Joe was still optimistic that it would be his last Christmas in captivity at Stalag Luft III. Being a relatively new Kriegie, he was aware of the latest advances that the Allies were carving out on both fronts, the Americans and British on the Western Front, and the Russians on the Eastern Front. He didn't see how the Germans could hang on much longer.

The Kriegies were organized in the same manner as if they were stationed at their respective home bases. The chain of command was recognized and respected. The German and Allied officers saluted each other. The ranking Allied officer was the German commandant's counterpart in all Kriegie matters. The Allied staff included a secret Escape Committee and a Security Group. The Escape Committee had the responsibility to review all escape plans and either put their stamp of approval on them, or deny them. If the committee approved a Kriegie's escape plan, it would provide the escapee all the aid and assistance it had at its disposal including passports and false ID's. If the committee disapproved the escape plan, the potential escapee was ordered not to attempt it.

Likewise, the Security Group was charged with the safeguard and proper dissemination of intelligence data. To assist them in their task, the Security Group had assembled a small radio from parts that were acquired by bribing certain guards to smuggle them into the Camp. There was no shortage of electronic engineers within the Kriegie population. The design and assembly of such a radio were not too difficult. It was used by the Security Group to record the daily broadcasts from the British Broadcasting Company (BBC). The BBC issued an accurate daily report of the progress of the war in the European Theater of Operations (ETO) as well as in the Pacific Theater of Operations (PTO). This data was then disseminated each evening to the Kriegie population in every barracks.

The handwritten news dispatches were usually carried from barracks to barracks in between the covers of a seemingly harmless book by a trusted security person. Upon the arrival of the news messenger, the barracks was put under a state of high security, and the news reader moved from room to room with his daily news updates. It was in this manner that the Kriegies were kept up to the minute with the progress of the war. It was this information that nourished their hopes and prayers for an early deliverance from their inhumane situation. And so each month, predictions for the end of the war were expressed with more and more hope. And indeed, the daily newscast information bore out that hope.

The most optimistic of the Kriegies dared to hope that they would be liberated by Christmas 1944, but on December 16, 1944, the Germans counter-attacked the Allies on the Western Front and caused many casualties in both deaths and prisoners taken. It was with the utmost strength and all-out efforts that the Allies were able to stem the Nazi offensive and retake the offensive in their march to Berlin. However, this battle, called the Battle of the Bulge, had a major effect in delaying the final victory by some three months. The Kriegies had to reset their timetables for liberation and prepared to endure still another winter as POW's.

The news of the Allied setback was received with grim faces and heavy hearts. But the courageous Kriegies had no doubt of the ultimate victory. They faced the Christmas of 1944 with a bittersweet resignation; they were still alive but they lived in a state of depressed physical deprivation and malnutrition.

Lovoi made it a habit to try to end his daily routine on a high note. Each night, after he had tucked himself into the bare accommodations of his bunk bed, fully clothed including his woolen cap pulled down over his ears, he carefully tore the paper cover from his semimonthly allotment of the Hershey chocolate bar that came in the Red Cross food parcel. He would break off one of the twelve pieces, but before he put it into his mouth, he sucked up any of the crumbs that might have chipped as a result of this procedure. Then he would place the chocolate square on the top of his tongue, moisten it slightly with his saliva, and vacuum it to the roof of his mouth, where he could slowly suck its melted pleasure at length. It was a challenge of sorts to see how long he could make the sweetness of that one piece of Hershey last. His swallows were few and far between. The object of this "game" was to fall asleep and swallow the last taste during a simultaneous moment. He could do this for twelve of the fifteen semi-monthly nights. On the other three nights, he struggled with the anticipated pleasure of the next twelve events.

It was on one of those three sugarless nights as he lay sleepless and restless on his hard bunk that his thoughts traveled across the devastated European continent, across the Atlantic Ocean, and entered the city of Cambridge, Massachusetts, settling at the kitchen table of his parents' colonial home at 104 Hancock Street. The atmosphere was unusually quiet for a normally vocal Italian immigrant family. His three unmarried sisters, Rosalie, Nerina, and Lauretta, were going about their activities almost in robotic fashion. His father, Ottavio, sat slumped in a kitchen chair, staring into empty space. His three brothers, Ben, Sam, and Sal, were away on military duty. Ben was fighting in the battle of Guadalcanal, Sam was on his way to Iwo Jima, and Sal was on submarine patrol with the Navy.

It didn't need a rocket scientist to sense that a pall of gloom lay upon the Lovoi household. Joe was MIA. He was last heard from on or about November 16, 1944. It was now approaching Christmastime and still no word from the War Department—not a good sign. Joe prayed that his brothers would safely endure the war and return home to a natural life. He remembered that the last time he saw his brother Sam bleeding, it was from a facial cut he sustained as he collided with a bleacher seat after being tackled in a football game. Sam was a halfback for the Auburn Football Team. Joe admired his brother Sam's athletic ability.

Ottavio, a wounded veteran of World War I, feared the worst. He had experienced the devastating residue of war. He knew that the chances of his son Joe, still being alive, were extremely slim. Joe's sisters, including his married sister, Anna, were religiously hoping that they would see their brother again but feared time might not be kind to their hopes.

Ottavio had slumped into a deep depression. He could not sit still. He could not sleep. He feared the worst. His experience as a WWI veteran told him that his son Joseph was dead. The small flicker of hope that he was wrong lay in the fact that Joseph's death was not yet confirmed by the War Department. These days he often could be found leaning on the gate in front of his yard on Hancock Street. He would turn his head to the right and notice that the fence had a definite bend in the middle of it caused by Joseph and his friends leaning on it while enjoying each other's company when they were just kids. On many occasions Ottavio would ask the boys to stop leaning on his fence and find some other place to congregate. Oh, how he rued those days. Oh, how he wished that Paul Kirby, Bobby Davidson, Howie Horton, Don McDougal, and George Minalga would come back home and lean on that fence again.

When learning of Joseph's missing in action status, Ottavio presented himself to the Military Recruiting Office in Boston and offered his services on the condition that he be shipped to the European Theater of Operations so he could look for his son, Joseph.

He pleaded his case and all but begged the recruiting officer to accept him. In his broken English, he explained that he would peel potatoes and cook for the American forces. He continued that he was an expert tailor and could sew the torn uniforms. Through his tears, he argued that he knew the territory and had the best chance of finding his son. He proudly showed the recruiting officer his U.S. Citizenship Certificate. His depression deepened when he was kindly rejected because of his age. He certainly did not lack the courage. He was fifty-six years old.

It was Joe's mother, Nancy, who constantly buoyed the spirits of the Lovoi family during those dark days. Nancy was a devout Catholic. Much of her life was spent in prayer and caring for the family requirements. It was she who spoke to her husband and children avowing that Joseph was alive and would return. And now that the Christmas season was upon them, Nancy continued a tradition that was begun by her son, Joseph, back in 1936 when the Lovois moved into their home on Hancock Street.

The home was a lovely colonial of Gothic design. The heavy oak door that separated the inner foyer from the outside faced a winding stairway that led to the second floor. It was a two-stage stairway with a landing halfway up. Just off this landing was a large closet-like grotto. It was wide and deep. Each Christmas season, Joseph would decorate this grotto with the nativity scene in Bethlehem, portraying the birth of the Christ Child. The centerpiece of this scene was a dimly lighted manger with miniature models of the Virgin Mary holding the Christ Child in her arms. In the immediate vicinity were such notables as Joseph, Gabriel, several other angels, a few sheep, and the Magi. Beyond the immediate vicinity there were unexplainable Christmas trees, lots of ground cover, a few stray sheep, and a camel or two. The grotto was ringed with a set of Christmas tree lights, which projected a cheerful scenario with varying shades of color throughout the grotto's enclosure.

Joe's mother made it a habit to pause at the mid-landing each time she had reason to climb or descend this front stairway. At every pause she would bless herself and momentarily meditate. It was on such an occasion that she knelt before the nativity scene. The Lovoi family was in its lowest state of depression. Nancy felt that she needed a miracle to assist her husband and children in overcoming their most difficult trial to date. She had the faith to overcome the situation, but she dearly wanted Ottavio and her daughters to have it too. As she fell to her knees, she looked into the face of the bowed head of the statue of Joseph and pleaded with him for a sign. She hesitantly whispered to the statue, "Is my son alive?"

Almost immediately, through her tear-stained eyes, she saw the statue of Joseph nod its head as a sign of affirmation. Joe's mother screamed and sank to the landing floor. Ottavio and Nerina ran from the kitchen to the stairway followed closely by Rosalie and Lauretta. They gathered around Nancy and asked what happened. When Nancy was able to regain her composure, she related the incident with the statue of Joseph. Nancy repeatedly screamed, "He's alive! He's alive!"

Of course, huddled in his cold bunk in Stalag Luft III, Joe could not have any knowledge that a miracle had notified his family that he was indeed alive. He closed his eyes and prayed for sleep. Mercifully, it came.

The days before Christmas dragged on, pulling with them an atmosphere of wishful optimism for the Christmas season and a guarded hopefulness for a safe and speedy liberation. The camp was busy. Food had been hoarded for weeks in anticipation of a Christmas "bash." Plans for elaborate meals were discussed each evening, with everyone pitching in with suggestions. The cook in

Joe's room had the talent not only to plan and cook a gourmet meal, but to give it a French name. For example, the supper for Christmas Day was Paté Cockerel. This was nothing more than canned chicken spread on a crispy cracker.

The "Brits" had a way of relating many of the incidents that occurred regarding their daily living habits to their normal living routines back home in England. The group of British flyers whom Joe and Nuffrie lived with were very pragmatic and practical in dealing with their situations. Most of them had been at the Stalag for more than two years. Each evening Nuffrie would strum his guitar and vocalize the more popular tunes. With Christmas on its way, lots of the tunes were seasonal, such as "White Christmas," "Jingle Bells," and many of the Christmas carols. The sing-a-long scenario was almost predictable. Nuffrie would sit on a chair in a corner of the room, blow warm breath on his cold fingers, and begin strumming. Joe and perhaps several other Kriegies from that room would find chairs and sit around Nuffrie, adding their voices to his.

Within a few minutes, the rest of the roommates would drop whatever they were doing and form several human sections of tenors, altos, and basses around Nuffrie until he was completely surrounded. The crescendo would rise to such a volume that it attracted many of the Kriegies from the other rooms in that barracks to drop by and join in. Sometimes the tunes would create an emotional mood within the chorus. Then every man would sing with his head staring straight ahead, for fear that the wetness under his eyes would be noticeable.

Even the German guards would peer into the room and poignantly smile their approval. There seemed to be

Nuffrie's musical band-aid

a cautious friendliness among the guards and the Kriegies during this season. It was a sentimental time of the year, one which now held hope for the Kriegies, but hopelessness for the Germans. Due to the shortage of German manpower, the prison guards were selected from the senior citizen age group. The younger men had to fill the combat roles. Lovoi could see the hidden despair in the guards' lined faces. He felt some pity for them.

It was Christmas Eve. The room occupied by Joe, Nuffrie, and the other sixteen "Brits" was unusually quiet. Each man was preoccupied in thought. Perhaps the occasion related their thoughts to other Christmases when there was peace and family. Lovoi was lying on his bunk with his eyes closed and his hat pulled down over his ears. For a moment he was back in the United States at an airfield in Virginia, named Langley Field. He had just completed his training as a radar navigator and was about to board a brand new B-17 Flying Fortress, just off the assembly line. It was named "Excalibur" after the sword of the legendary King Arthur.

Lovoi and his crew were getting ready to fly this B-17 to Europe to add its potential devastating role to that of the 463rd Bomb Group in Foggia, Italy. The route to be flown included stops at Grenier Field, New Hampshire; Goose Bay, Canada; the Azores, Portugal; Marrakech, Morocco; Tunis, Tunisia; and Foggia, Italy. Since Joe was the navigator on this extended flight, he had some leeway as to the flight plans. The leg from Langley Field, Virginia, to Grenier Field, New Hampshire, just happened to cross the state of Massachusetts via the city of Cambridge.

Joe's family lived in Cambridge. He had called his mother the day before his flight and told her that if she, and as many members of the family as she could round

112

up, would happen to be in her back yard at about 1:00 P.M. the next day, they would be in for a very pleasant surprise. And so it was that on the next day, upon reaching cruising altitude on "Excalibur," Lovoi gave the pilot the heading to Grenier Air Field in New Hampshire via Cambridge, Massachusetts. The pilot was very cooperative in helping Joe to accomplish his personal mission.

The home where Joe and his family lived was located just off of Massachusetts Avenue, which bridged the colleges of Harvard and Massachusetts Institute of Technology. As the pilot approached Cambridge, he gradually reduced the B-17's altitude to the point where the altimeter read, 1,000 feet as it swooped over the Harvard Yard and made a beeline along Massachusetts Avenue eastward to MIT. Halfway there Joe pointed out the yellow colonial home on Hancock Street just off of Massachusetts Avenue. There, standing and waving in the back yard of number 104 were Joe's mother, father, and two of his sisters. As the huge bomber roared its presence over Joe's home, the pilot rocked the wings, revved the four powerful engines, and pulled "Excalibur" up into a steep climb. He did not level it off until he reached 5,000 feet and was on course to Grenier Field, New Hampshire. In the stillness of that cold room in Stalag Luft III, Joe relived that once in a lifetime memory and wondered.

True to his promise, the Australian cook was able to put together a five-course meal on Christmas Day. With the tins of chicken, turkey, and tuna that he had been able to squirrel away for the past several months, he came up with the following menu:

Breakfast: Porrage Semoline
              Sardine au toast
              Thé

Lunch:	Sausage au pain frite
	Fromage au pain frite
	Café

Tea:	Honne au toast
	Gateau noeloise
	Thé

Dinner:	Hors d'oeuvres
	Emendve soup
	Turké
	Bonbons
	Café

Supper:	Paté cockerel
	Fromage au toast
	Cocoa

The only thing missing from this "feast" was the seasonal setting, such as might be seen at one of the elegant dining cafés on the Champs Elysées in Paris.

For this very special occasion, all members of Joe's room bathed and shaved, even in the icy conditions. They wore their cleanest outfits. There were smiles, handshakes, optimistic remarks, happy greetings, and warm embraces. It was an emotional day. They tried to be happy, but it was difficult to do so in the face of the bleak months ahead. For most the day, Nuffrie sat in a corner of the room and rhythmically strummed his guitar, filling the room with light airs and soft background chords. He seemed pleased as the Kriegies complimented him. He smiled at their nods of approval and even blushed as he realized he was the center of attraction. He was able to fill most of their requests. The music seemed to make the gloom vanish from the room. It was Christmas Day and eighteen closely knit Kriegies were about to sit down for their Christmas meal. Only God knew when and where their next Christmas Day would be spent. This was the one day of his entire six-month prison stay that Lovoi's belly would be filled. This was the sixth week of his captivity.

The weather for the Christmas season 1944 was cold and moisture laden. The precipitation was in the form of snow and sometimes a mixture of snow and sleet. Except for the required head count during the *appels,* most of the Kriegies stayed indoors. Some of the more hardy souls and more recent Kriegies did take short walks on the restricted paths at the perimeter of the camp.

After supper was over, the socializing continued into the early evening. Kriegies from other barracks did brave the elements to exchange greetings with their fellow Kriegies. The POW's were experiencing emotional feelings, which were amplified when Nuffrie began to strum his guitar again. Christmas carols seemed to be the favorite tunes. Nearly all of the Kriegies knew most of them. Then came "I'm Dreaming of a White Christmas." The mood sobered somewhat as the refrain "May your day be merry and bright. And may all your Christmases be white," wafted its way around the room. Finally, the chef was singled out and pushed into the center of a circle composed of the other seventeen Kriegies. The circle clapped hands and sang "For he's a jolly good fellow." The last phrase of that song "That nobody can deny" was the signal that the evening of food and comradery was over. Nuffrie put his guitar away for the night, and the Kriegies melted silently into their bunks, physically spent.

The rest of December 1944 was like a lost weekend. The remaining days blended into each other, leaving no significant imprint on the lives of the Kriegies. The weather grew colder, the days seemed to be grayer, and the larder was lower, thanks to the Christmas "bash." A recent BBC news report gave support that the war was winding down and should be over by this time next year. And so the Kriegies took some comfort in the thought that as each day passed, they would enjoy that same day, next year, in freedom, peace, and in pursuit of their dreams.

Cold and hunger, two of the three most feared enemies of the Kriegies, took their positions within the Stalag. The third enemy, fear, lived within each Kriegie's heart and managed to increase its pump rate every now and then. The temperature had dropped below freezing and stayed there for the rest of December. The recent newscasts were somewhat disheartening. The Allies were licking their wounds as a result of the Battle of the Bulge. After stemming the German tide, the Allies were regrouping for their next assault as they drove to capture Berlin. The safety and fate of the POW's throughout Germany were still in doubt.

Rumors that Hitler had ordered his generals to execute all POW's, unless the Allies reconsidered their ultimatum for peace from "unconditional" surrender to "conditional" surrender, added to the confusion that was beginning to show up at Stalag Luft III. The Russian armies were advancing on the Eastern Front and their artillery fire could be seen from the POW camp at Sagan.

Quickly, the last day of December 1944 became New Year's Eve. Lovoi's room had become unusually quiet. Maybe it was too cold to carry on a conversation, or maybe it was just the emotional letdown from the Christmas high. But whatever it was, Nuffrie put an end to it when he slipped over to his favorite corner of the room and began to aimlessly strum his guitar. At first he played just chords, any chords that sounded pleasant. And then the chords seemed to meld into recognizable tunes. It started with "Waltzing Matilda." Everyone in the room perked up. They sang it over and over again, each time the volume increased. Lovoi and Brancato enjoyed listening to the loud male chorus with strong British accents, as they sang themselves out of breath. And then there was a lull.

Nuffrie softly strummed the opening phrases of "Auld Lang Syne." The room became very serious as he continued to play this unforgettable tune. The men hummed the first few lines, "Should auld acquaintance be forgot and never brought to mind?" As they were humming these lines, they were forming a human ring. They clasped each other's hands until the human bond was complete, except for Nuffrie. And then Nuffrie began again, "Should auld acquaintance be forgot?" This time the voices sang the words that blended into an emotional melody and continued all the way through to "We'll take a cup of kindness yet," and then the last line "For auld lang syne."

The men were on their feet as they sang and turned to each other with lusty voices and determined, red-eyed expressions. They sang the song for a second time. This time it was much louder. It was a wonder that the roof on the barracks was not blown off to let the Berliners know how the Kriegies felt about each other. And then it was over. The new year was at hand. The room became very quiet and still as the Kriegies sought their bunks to privatize their emotional silence. Soon most of them sank into a restless sleep.

117

VIII
A Forced March to Hope

During the middle and end of January, 1945, the Allies were regrouping and solidifying their resources on the Western Front in preparation for a decisive blow at the German heartland. According to the recent BBC newscast received by the clandestine radio at the Stalag, the Allies were predicting total victory by the spring of that year. Additionally, something ominous was brewing along the Eastern Front. German resistance was cracking all along the Eastern Front. The Russian army was a vengeful one. It had a long memory concerning the German army atrocities during their invasion of Russia. Not many prisoners were being taken.

The war along the Eastern Front was important to the Kriegies in Stalag Luft III because their camp was in the direct line of the Russian advance to Berlin. The sweetest revenge that the Russian army could taste would be to capture Berlin before the Americans and British arrived. The Kriegies had mixed emotions about the possibility of being liberated by the Russian army. Adolf Hitler had not made up his mind whether to release the Kriegies to the oncoming Russians, or to evacuate them and hold them hostage as negotiating pawns, or to cage them and locate them in target areas such as Berlin.

While the Germans were deliberating this dilemma, the Russian army kept inching its way westward. On some clear nights, the Kriegies could see the artillery flashes on the distant eastern horizon, followed by the rumble produced by the explosions. The German commandant of the camp wasted no more time. He issued orders to the Allied senior officer of the South Camp to prepare the Kriegies to evacuate the camp and march within thirty minutes. When this information was relayed to the POW's, the air became electrified with excitement. The weather was extremely cold. The men were ill prepared for such an undertaking. They had no winter clothes, a short food supply, and their malnutritioned bodies would be unable to sustain the rigors of such a trek. But, of course they had no say in the decision except to prepare as best they could to be ready as the marching orders for each camp were issued.

It was decided to gather all of the bulk food in the larder and mix it in several ways in order to cook meals that could be divided into eighteen portions so each Kriegie could manage his own diet. Meats were baked into meat pies. Fish was gathered and cooked into fish cakes. Powdered milk, sugar, cocoa, and barley were all mixed together and baked into a highly nutritious cake that was cut into eighteen pieces. And so it went.

The Kriegies did their best to prepare for the worst. Makeshift back packs were strung together for ease of toting necessary belongings. Heavy items were destined to be left behind. No Kriegie was to travel alone. The buddy system was to be employed throughout. Of course, Joe and Nuffrie were paired as buddies and worked on a travel plan that would maximize their combined energies. Stalag Luft III had a population of about ten thousand Allied POW's. The marching formation was carefully drawn up by the combined efforts of the Allied senior officer and the German commandant's staff. The prisoners had to be counted as they exited the camp. It was calculated that given the conditions, namely, snow, freezing temperature, and the late hour, it would take about eight hours to completely evacuate the prison camp and create a parade of marching Kriegies nearly twenty miles long. But the order was given to march and march they did. It was 3:45 A.M. on January 28, 1945, when the North Camp was ordered to move. Lovoi and Brancato lowered their heads and joined the ranks of Kriegies heading for the Stalag's barbed-wire gate after the completion of the head count. The camp lights were on in an effort to assist the German guards to herd the POW's into some kind of marching formation. The lights swept the camp and revealed the armed tower guards as they overlooked the activity.

At last the North Camp was in formation and ready to march. The biting wind was blowing the sleet in a strong west-to-east direction. Its intensity could be measured by the nearly horizontal direction it was coming from. The Kriegie formation had become somewhat straggled as it passed through the prison gates under escort of dozens of guards on either side of the formation. Lovoi and his buddy were about twenty-five rows back from the front of the formation. Their way was pretty well trampled by the time they sloshed through the precipitated snowfall.

There must have been at least a foot of snow and sleet over which the formation of Kriegies had to tramp. And the conditions did not get any better as the quivering mass of humanity left Sagan and entered the unknown and dark vacuum that lay ahead. Hour after hour they plodded through the blackness of the night, a blizzard

Escape from Russian advance

A forced march to nowhere

swirling around them, winds driving near-zero temperatures through their very bones.

The only way to march without getting their heads frozen was for the POW's to bend at the waist, twist their shoulders into the wind, and bow their heads forward, into the teeth of the freezing gale. Every once in a while, they would look up to get their bearings, and then resume the bent and bowed position. The going was tough. The progress was slow. The Kriegies kept silent to save their energy for the task ahead, surviving the elements. It was the morning of January 28, 1945. The next three hours were spent in putting as much distance as possible between Stalag Luft III and the weary Kriegie column. For the most part, only the wind and the rhythmic snow crunching sounds of the plodding army of human beings was heard. Except for an occasional cough, silence was kept throughout the herded POW's. Then, the weaving column came to the edge of a forest, which lay in their path.

The German commander gave the order to halt. The Kriegies welcomed the relief. They were ordered to "fall out," find a likely spot, and rest for twenty minutes. All of the Kriegies melted into the woods and tried to find a tree that would protect them from the wind. They sat on the snow and broke out some of their precious food reserves. They were careful to eat and drink sparingly, not knowing what the future would hold in store for them.

The order to "fall in" came sooner than expected. It was still snowing hard. The South Camp was in the vanguard of the five camps that made up Stalag Luft III. Lovoi and Brancato were near the front rows of Kriegies from the North Camp, but far enough back of them so they did not have to plod through any virgin snowfall. They tried to walk in the footsteps of those human rows ahead of them. When the march resumed, Joe maintained his head-bowed position, hands in pockets, and shoulders into the wind. By now his shoes and feet were frozen. The path being plowed by the retreating Kriegies looked like a giant caterpillar squirming its way through the snow-covered fields. The parade left a wide trail of hard-packed snow, which eventually turned into a slippery icy path. The snow kept falling into the night and early morning. The winds became omni-directional, blowing the snow in swirling designs. Finally, the snowfall abated. It was early morning and the sun was trying to peek through the weather as if to inspect the damage caused by the storm. Its reflection from the white ground cover caused the Kriegies to squint and shade their eyes. The wind continued to be a debilitating factor as it chilled noses and uncovered cheeks. The now ragged parade of POW's was spaced at certain intervals between horse-drawn wagons. The wagons were used to haul Kriegies and guards who could not keep up with the pace, or who fell ill and could not walk, or who were dead.

It was now nearly ten hours since the evacuation had begun. The Kriegies needed to be rested. The advance had slowed considerably as the men grew weaker. The march commanders, observing the slowdown and the reasons for it, gave the order to take a fifteen-minute break. The Kriegies were told that they would be arriving at their first rest stop within a few hours. During this break, the men ate sparingly and stuffed their mouths with clean snow. This slaked their thirst and improved their spirits.

Again, the men were reassembled into a march formation and continued to plod. Joe twisted his head toward a passing wagon. He was somewhat surprised to see several prone bodies lying on the wagon bed. The

The marching Kriegies take a break

bodies were still. And now that the snowstorm was over, the Kriegies walked taller. They kept forging forward walking in mechanical style like wound-up robots. By midday, the weary column had arrived at a small town called by the name of Fretwaldau. It was virtually split in two sections by a main street that was too narrow for the column to negotiate without making some adjustments.

On the other side of this town, there was a large dairy farm with half a dozen large barns that were situated within short walking distance of each other. Most of them were empty. They had been used to store farm machinery, produce, and dairy products. Now they sheltered just a few cows, other farm animals, and winter vegetables. The German command gave the order to "fall out" and find shelter within these buildings. They were warned not to damage or destroy any of the facilities. This last remark brought sarcastic smiles to some of the men's faces. One of them was heard to mumble under his breath, "Yeah, practice what you preach."

The column of POW's broke abruptly as they sought refuge and haven in the barns. It got a little unruly as the men tried to get into comfortable sitting and lying positions and make room for the rest of the troops. By the time Lovoi and Brancato were able to enter one of the barns, most of the choice spots were taken. There was just enough room for two more men at the bottom of a huge pile of rutabagas (turnips). Joe scavenged some straw while Nuffrie held the spots. Finally, the two friends sat beside each other and assessed their conditions. They were indeed very tired, cold, and very hungry. But they were still alive and full of hope that things would get better. They dared not take their shoes off to warm their frozen feet, since they were warned that they would not be able to put them back on.

While in the act of lying down and getting comfortable, the Kriegie next to Nuffrie accidentally dislodged a key rutabaga. This caused about a dozen rutabagas to come toppling down on the Kriegies who were seated at the base of the pile. One of the falling vegetables hit Nuffrie on the side of his head and knocked him nearly unconscious. He was quite hurt and dazed. Joe ran outside to gather a large snowball. He quickly pressed it against the injured side of Nuffrie's head and held it in place. He sat next to Nuffrie and cradled his bruised head into his lap, all the while holding the snowball against it. This first aid kept the swelling down and relieved the pain. Nuffrie expressed a low moan, turned over on his side, and was soon asleep on Joe's lap. Joe carefully looked for signs of bleeding. There were none. He then covered Nuffrie with a blanket and went looking for water.

The water supply for the farmhouse was provided by a hand-operated well that was situated just behind it. The well was under guard by an armed German. There was no way that it could provide enough water to satisfy the ten thousand Kriegies. The Kriegies were given permission to have small fires for the purpose of melting snow, cooking their food, and brewing tea and coffee. The fires were to be limited and well controlled. Nuffrie was still sleeping, so Joe went in search of firewood.

He came upon a large wooden barrel, open at the top. He peered in and saw that it contained what looked like cold milk. Even though it was bluish in color, Joe decided to taste it. He gripped the edge of the barrel with both hands and swung his upper body into the barrel. When his mouth reached the contents, he drank heavily. He drew back in an upright position and swallowed. It tasted sour and almost made him throw up. He wiped his mouth on his sleeve and backed away from the barrel. Just then a passing Kriegie informed him that he had taken a drink from the pigs' supply of milk. The thought of becoming infected with tuberculosis did cross his mind, but there was no room for it among all his other problems for that moment.

It was early evening when the Kriegies were given the order to prepare to march within the next hour. Although the thought of facing the elements again was somewhat disheartening, they did want to get going and reach wherever their destination was to be so they could settle down. And so with mixed emotions, they put on their thin outdoor clothing and gathered their belongings. Nuffrie seemed to be okay except for a headache.

The food and rest did refresh the POW's and prepared them for the next leg of their march to nowhere. The temperature was well below freezing, but the storm was over. Had the temperature been above freezing, the marching conditions would have been a lot worse due to the slipping and sliding induced by melting snow. Joe and Nuffrie were marching side by side, making small talk, and lifting each other's spirit. They were heard to gasp occasionally as the cold wind found any kind of opening between their coat collars and necks. Necks were not the only targets of the relentless wind. Joe's fingers began to freeze, his toes had no feeling left in them, and his frozen face made it hard for him to speak in an articulate manner.

Slowly but surely the undulating column of frozen Kriegies ground out the distance. Every now and then, another victim of exhaustion was picked up by the guards and placed in the horse-drawn wagons. The more fortunate ones looked on with sad expressions, wondering what fate awaited their fallen comrades. The rest of that day passed by without further consequences. Except for the occasional rest break and snacking, the Kriegies kept to the march in silence.

It was now early evening and the sun had begun to set. There was no precipitation that day, only cold blustery winds. Then faintly on the western horizon, there appeared a sky glow that attracted the attention of all the Kriegies. As the column continued to proceed toward it, the glow grew brighter and spread across most of the cloudless sky. It was the reflection of moonlight that caused the glow and it seemed to be centered over the next rest stop. The stop was the city of Muskau, Germany.

Muskau was an urban manufacturing center where most of the country's tile was manufactured. As the POW's marched into the outskirts of the city, they could see countless numbers of abandoned factories and office buildings, which had once housed large numbers of workers who produced the ceramic products. The Kriegies were ordered to find shelter in these buildings and bed down for the night. This move took them out of the wind and weather.

Although the temperature inside was still below the freezing mark, the change from outdoors to indoors provided a welcomed warmth. Nuffrie's head wound was better and his headache was gone. He and Joe found a dry spot on the factory floor and placed their blankets on it. They sat down, Indian style, and dug into their dwindling provisions. They munched on the last of the all-purpose cake that the cook had baked prior to their departure from Stalag Luft III and then split a small can of deviled ham. There was no drinking water for either straight consumption, or with which to brew tea or coffee. So, the meal was eaten and swallowed dry. Shortly after they finished their meal, they lay down to rest and fell into a fitful sleep.

They awoke early the next morning and stretched their sore muscles. In spite of the cold, they were able to restore most of their blood circulation. Some of the more adventurous Kriegies dared to leave the building to meet with some of the residents of Muskau. They were quite willing to trade water and bread for American cigarettes. When these Kriegies returned to the factory with their spoils of food and water, other Kriegies felt brave enough to do the same. This trading went on for some time before the guards got wind of it. Before the angry guards were able to put a stop to this bartering, Joe and Nuffrie were fortunate to trade two packs of cigarettes for two glasses of water. The guards reprimanded the Muskau residents for their behavior, which was tantamount to collaboration with the enemy. By the looks of expression on the faces of the residents, who by now had lined the sidewalks on the main street, this admonishment fell on deaf ears. Muskau is located about thirty-seven miles west of Sagan.

The Kriegies were in pretty bad physical condition by the time they reached Muskau. They were coughing, sneezing, damp, and shivering. The Allied officer in charge of the POW's thought it was time to make some reasonable demands. He met with the German commandant and insisted on knowing where the Kriegies were being taken and how much longer they would have to bear the terribly inhumane conditions. He argued that his men were weak and exhausted and needed some encouraging news. The Commandant explained that the Kriegies were headed for a city called Spremberg, where they would be boarded onto a train to another prison camp, out of harm's way. They would be transported to one of two available camps, Nurnberg or Moosburg. Both camps were located near the city of Munich, Germany.

The march to Spremberg from Muskau was delayed several more days due to lack of transportation from the Spremberg railroad station. It would take some time to assemble the necessary engines and cars to move nearly ten thousand Kriegies once they arrived at Spremberg. And so it was more practical to keep the Kriegies at Muskau where they had living quarters, albeit poor, rather than have them stay in open fields adjacent to the railroad station. However, the Kriegies were on their own as far as food and water were concerned. By now their food supplies were nearly exhausted.

It snowed quite heavily for the next two days, which was a mixed blessing for the POW's. On the one hand, the snowfall provided a source of clean water, but on the other hand, the added snow would make the going harder to march through. At last, the Kriegies were ordered to fall out and form into a column of sixes, ready to march. It was necessary, however, to reduce the column width so that the formation could fit through the town's main street. On the way out, the Kriegies waved to the civilian crowd that had gathered on the sidewalks out of curiosity. The crowd's mood was not unfriendly. They waved back at the Kriegies. The mutual waving was a hopeful sign of things to come.

As the marching prisoners exited the town to the west, they were ordered to resume the six-abreast formation that they had formed when leaving Stalag Luft III. The day was crisp, with a layer of high thin clouds. There was very little wind, but the temperature was still flirting about the freezing point. The march from Muskau to Spremberg spanned the time from mid-morning to late afternoon. The Kriegies began the march relatively refreshed from their two-day rest, but by the time they reached the Spremberg railroad station, they were exhausted. The horse-drawn wagons with their sick and dying human cargo were last seen as the horses plodded their way from the railroad station toward the outskirts of the town, hopefully, to a hospital.

The railroad station consisted of several passenger terminals with a spacious snow-covered emptiness in the rear, which might have served as a parking lot at one time. The waiting rooms faced the platform where the trains stopped to pick up passengers and cargo. There seemed to be no bomb damage to this railroad depot, indicating perhaps that it was not a military target.

Upon their arrival at the Spremberg railroad station, the POW's were herded into the large snow-covered field to the rear of the terminal buildings. The few German passersby turned their heads in curiosity. They had never seen such a spectacle, ten thousand young men, gathered in such a large group, smoking and milling around waiting for some troop transport trains. The Kriegies were given water from several large buckets pulled through the assembly on sleds by German guards. There was lots of coughing and some vomiting. The POW's were not in the best of health. Some of them needed immediate medical attention. The German commandant promised that the trains would arrive shortly and begin their journey south to either Nurnberg or Moosburg. And so they waited and waited. The little sun that they had seen all day had now set.

The daylight began to fade and still there were no trains to be seen. The men grew restless. They were cold and many of them had used up all their food. Lovoi and Brancato edged their way through the crowd toward the terminal buildings. When they had reached them, they found some relief by leaning against the cold walls and taking some weight off their frozen feet. Some of the Kriegies were actually sitting down against the buildings even though they were sitting on snow-covered ground.

At last the sound of a train whistle was heard off in the distance. There was still no sign of the train, but the whistle grew louder. The German guards ran off the platform to clear the tracks of any Kriegies who might not have heard the train whistle. And then a giant black steam-driven engine came into sight. It was pulling on what appeared to be an endless number of box cars that might have been twenty-five years old. The shock and disappointment that the POW's felt at that moment was just a prelude of shocks and disappointments to come.

The German guards pushed and shoved the Kriegies onto the box cars, filling them one at a time. They counted fifty men to a car plus one German armed guard. There was no room for sitting, let alone lying down for the sick. The men were crammed in standing positions. Of course it took some time for the total number of box cars to be filled. While some Kriegies were freezing on the platform, waiting to be packed out of the wind, the Kriegies who were squeezed into the initial box cars were beginning to perspire from the body heat of the crammed and crushed fifty passengers.

There were four trains in all, each carrying about 2,500 prisoners. As each trainload was filled, the train took off, heading south on its inhumane journey to hell. The conditions were so bad that each box car quickly selected a leader to direct and supervise the behavior of the Kriegies in that box car so that the suffering could be tolerated. For example, the Kriegies' position in the box car was changed every hour so that those Kriegies in the

Fetid boxcars transport Kriegies to Stalag VII A

outer part of the group would work their way toward the center of the group, shedding the cold box car walls for the warm bodies in the middle of the group. And those Kriegies in the middle of the group were moved from the hot bodies center of the group toward the cold walls of the box cars that made up the perimeter of the group of fifty.

Further, when one or more of the Kriegies got sick, they were placed in a prone position somewhere between the center of the group and the outside periphery of the group. The fact that the box cars were very old was a blessing because their splintered walls leaked ventilation into the dark and musty speeding human freight carrier. The Kriegies tried very hard to keep their composure, and most of them succeeded. But those who suffered from claustrophobic symptoms had a hard time of it. They were given as much consideration as possible from the rest of the carload of Kriegies. For example, they were spoken to and calmed down by the cooler heads in the group.

Lovoi felt just as close and anxious as the rest of them. He would close his eyes, grit his teeth, and remind himself that each minute that passed diminished the time that he and his comrades had to suffer the pain and indignities of this latest phase of his life as a prisoner of war. Up to this point, he had been waging a battle to be as fastidious as possible, even to the point where he would take frequent cold (freezing) water baths in the Stalag Luft III latrine. He brushed his teeth regularly, shaved his face, and washed his underclothing at every opportunity. But now, he was helpless to continue those efforts.

The men were penned up like animals. There was little they could do regarding the normal bodily functions that were unavoidable. The boxcars stank. The train stopped twice each day and allowed the prisoners to exit their box cars in a controlled manner. This gave them the opportunity to attend to some of their bodily functions, because the train always stopped somewhere out in the deserted countryside. At these rest stops, the box car's floors were swept of feces and vomit that had accumulated since its last stop.

The entire trip from Spremberg to Moosburg, a distance of approximately four hundred miles, took nearly a day and a half. This was due to a zig-zag route that the train had to travel as it avoided the Allied bombings of railroad facilities as well as necessary stops during clear weather when the train literally had to hide from the Allied fighter aircraft that were roaming the enemy land, looking for targets of opportunity. But somehow, the box cars full of sick and debilitated Kriegies did arrive at the Moosburg railroad station.

The freight doors were opened that late afternoon of February 8, 1945, and the Kriegies jumped and tumbled out of their living nightmare into a sweet-smelling crispy atmosphere. As Joe looked around him and noted the long row of buses waiting to carry him and his comrades to another prison camp, Stalag VII-A, he felt the irony of looking forward to the next phase of his captivity. He knew it had to be better than the train ride from Spremberg to Moosburg. That had to be one of the low points of the POW experience. Yet, once again, it spurred the Kriegies on to heroic behavior, exhibiting bravery, stamina, patriotism, and guts.

In military-like manner, this bedraggled mass of displaced Allied male youths lined up, were counted, and marched to the waiting buses. It was a quiet procession. The men were sick and exhausted. The bus ride to Stalag

Stalag VII A: Kriegie Check-in

VII-A was a short one. The camp was constructed similar to Stalag Luft III but was in much worse condition. It had the double-barbed-wire fencing, the high wooden watchtowers with their machine gun emplacements, the wide barbed-wire gate, and the checkpoint shed. Lovoi could see beyond the fencing the low gray wooden barracks that lined up in rows about fifty feet apart. It was a cold late afternoon and most of the Kriegies who were already residents of Stalag VII-A were poking their heads out of their barracks windows to catch a glimpse of the new arrivals.

Whenever new arrivals were admitted to a camp, there usually was a flurry of shuffling POW's looking for lost buddies. Sometimes this activity met with great emotional success as the buddies hugged each other, and sometimes this activity prolonged the misery of still not knowing the fate of some of the airmen who were last seen as they parachuted earthward over enemy territory.

The barracks were smaller than those in Stalag Luft III. The Germans placed twelve Kriegies to a room, filled with four each three-tiered bunk beds. The bunk beds were so close to each other that the Kriegies could not sit up on their bunks. There was no head room. There was no heat of course and the conditions were generally miserable. The bunk beds were full of fleas and lice, food was scarce, and there were no medical facilities. It seemed that every POW was on his own. Each had to figure out ways to stay alive, cook what food he was given by the Germans with the dwindling supply of Red Cross parcels.

Stalag VII-A was the catch-all prison camp for those Kriegies who had to be evacuated by the Germans as a result of the Russian advance in the East and the American advance in the West. Therefore, there was very little discipline as the crowded facility became even more crowded in the days to come. The spring thaw came early. The camp grounds became very muddy. There were puddles everywhere. Morale was very low. The Kriegies lived from day to day, expecting at any moment the American advance would reach Moosburg and free them.

Due to the disorganized state of Stalag VII-A, some of the new arrivals were placed in a small compound consisting of four stables with dirt floors. Lovoi and Brancato were two of the unlucky ones who were quartered there. The Germans said it was a temporary measure until some of the barracks were made ready for inhabitants. The worst was yet to come.

As spring arrived in Bavaria, some of the Kriegies moved out of the barracks, and into tents that had been erected to accommodate the steady stream of evacuees from other stalags throughout Germany. The camp began to resemble a giant hobo village. Sanitary conditions were unbearable. The Stalag was built to house 14,000 POW's. At its peak occupancy, it held 130,000 prisoners.

Appels were still observed twice a day, although the Germans did not have a clue as to the accurate count.

Stalag VII A: domesticated Kriegies

A grim picture

Overcrowding forces Kriegies to find elbow room in tents

Laundry time

Kriegies trying to forget reality

Abominable latrine conditions

IX

A Comrade from the Grave

The German guards unceremoniously herded a group of about five hundred POW's into the stable compound. They were given bales of hay to spread on the ground and use this cover as bedding. The overcrowded stable compound did not provide enough room for all of the men to sleep at one time. So, they slept in shifts, packed like sardines, head to toe, and somehow managed to maintain their sanity. The poor living conditions were aggravated when a long slit trench had to be dug to serve as a common open-air latrine.

It was still winter in Moosburg, and its chill hung in the air. The use of this trench was just less than torture. Many times the POW's got sick and ran to the trench. Often they did not make it on time. This resulted in vomit being deposited just outside the door of the stable compound, making night use of the latrine a careful tiptoe and balancing act. Dysentery was rampant throughout the POW population. The line-up for the use of this crude facility was endless.

Water was supplied by several one-hundred-gallon tanks. It was used for drinking and washing. Food, of course, was scarce. What little food the Kriegies were doled was barely fit for human consumption. But the will to live was greater than the tendency to starve. Most of what was doled out was made from dehydrated vegetables into a green soup. The Germans added black bread slices thinly coated with margarine and a suspicious blood sausage. These five hundred Kriegies spent the rest of February, 1945, living under these most miserable conditions.

It took nearly two days to transfer the Kriegies from the stable compound into regular barracks. The Germans first searched them for articles of contraband and escape. Then they deloused them and their clothing, and had each Kriegie take a shower. It was somewhat of a shock to see the naked flea-bitten, skeletal bodies with red welts and scratches all over them. The real consequences of the long forced march and the stable life could now be observed. Yet, the Kriegies had a determined look in their eyes in defiance of the German treatment. They had something to look forward to if they survived this ordeal. The American Dream was still capable of being realized. But the German guards had nothing to look forward to. Their country was losing the war and most of them had nothing to go back to. Their country was devastated, their leadership was nonexistent, and their wills were dead.

The "cleaned up" barracks, which Lovoi and his comrades were moved into, were anything but "cleaned up." The bed bunks had flea and lice-infested straw, the floors were filthy, and the windows were hardly transparent. It did not make sense to be deloused and then be moved into barracks that were flea-infested. This was just one example of how disorganized the German POW staff was. Some of the bunk beds were not fully assembled yet, forcing Lovoi and Brancato, among others, to sleep on the floor temporarily. The bunk beds were assembled in tiers of four each, with common sides to save space and material. The bunks were spaced so close together that it was impossible for the Kriegies to sit up in their bunks. The barracks consisted of sleeping quarters, kitchens with wood-burning stoves, and wash rooms. The use of the stoves was guided by the availability of fuel.

So, there were not many hot dishes at Stalag VII-A. Moving into Stalag VII-A was like starting Kriegie life all over again. The facilities were very primitive and limited. It was estimated that the Stalag housed upwards of 130,000 POW's of all nationalities, American, British, French, Italian, Russian, and Slavs. It had originally been designed to care for about one-tenth that number.

When the kitchen stoves became obsolete due to lack of fuel, each Kriegie was left to his own devices as to how to heat his food and brewing water. The Germans were having their own food problems. The Red Cross food parcels stopped coming from Switzerland due to the fighting going on in the sector between Switzerland and Munich. The Allies were pushing the German Army north and east into the arms of the oncoming Russian Army, which was mopping up the same German Army from the Eastern Front. The Red Cross food parcels were substituted for with rations of barley and sauerkraut. The sauerkraut caused many of the Kriegies to vomit if eaten in large amounts. There was no rationing of sauerkraut. It came in large wooden barrels and was placed in convenient locations throughout the camp for easy access. Lovoi could stomach it in small quantities without getting sick.

But American ingenuity came to the rescue. Some bright Kriegie invented a small stove made from empty klim cans. Powdered klim (milk spelled backwards) was found in the Red Cross parcels. This small stove could reach very high intense temperatures using only slivers of wood as fuel. It worked on some obscure principle that the gaseous element of the wood fire combustion was flammable when mixed with fresh air. In any event, it worked.

The stove was made from two empty tin cans full of nail holes, one smaller than the other. The smaller can was nailed in the center of the larger tin can. The larger tin can had a flat top to it for placement of small pots and pans. The flat tops were also constructed out of tin cans. It also was designed to have an adjustable vent control. And so, the Kriegies built these stoves by the hundreds. It usually took two Kriegies to cook a meal, one to hold the potted meal over the fire, and one to feed the fire with small slivers of wood, about the size of matchsticks.

These marvelous stoves used very little fuel and operated at a very high efficiency to provide an almost blow-torch-like flame. The major problem with this newly discovered heating technique was the scarcity of wood for fuel. There was no loose wood to be had for love or money. Yet every evening the camp was filled with the smell of smoke emitted by these hundreds of stoves. Hundreds of Kriegies were bent over every evening as they cooked whatever food they had. They were cooking up a storm.

The German guards were perplexed because they were unable to figure out where the wood fuel was coming from. But if they were to look under the bunk bed straw mattresses, they would count only five wooden slats to support its occupants, not six. And as the days wore on, if they were to measure the width of the remaining five bed slats, they would be surprised to learn that they had shrunk from three inches, to two. And as more time wore on, if they were to inspect the joists of the barracks roof, they would be amazed to find that their upper sides were whittled to a smaller size. And so it went. The Kriegies were always able to find small slivers of wood to fuel their tin can cooking stoves.

Of course, in the long run, even the Goons (German Guards) were able to figure out where the wood was coming from. They were angry and embarrassed! They were furious! They demanded an immediate meeting with the senior Allied officer. The German commandant threatened harsh penalties if the practice of "razing" the barracks continued. The Allied officer agreed to order his men to cooperate and obey the German edict. But the undaunted Kriegies found new places to whittle, places that the guards would not find until the war was over. They began to slice away at the underside of the floor boards and the underside of the door panels. And if the Goons were to casually measure the height of the kitchen tables, they would be astonished to learn that they had shrunk about an inch.

As March spilled its way into April, the Allies and the Russians were getting closer to Moosburg. The Goons now had more to worry about than where the wood slivers were coming from. The Kriegies began to get excited as they sensed liberation. The positions of the Allied Forces were marked on an outdoor map provided by the German staff for the Kriegies to track the battle lines. They were marked in red on a lucite sheet taped over a map of Eastern Europe. The daily changes on this presentation were verified by the updates that the Kriegies were receiving, as a result of the nightly BBC newscasts, which arrived on the clandestine radio. The German version of the location of the battle lines was underplayed for an Allied advance and overplayed for a German counterattack.

It was while looking at this map that Lovoi received the shock of his life. He was studying the opposing positions and like a good navigator, he tried to calculate the

Kriegies cooking on tin can stoves

number of days it would take for the Allied Forces to reach Stalag VII-A, given the rate of advance admitted by the Germans. Suddenly, he heard a loud voice yell, "Hey, Lovoi, do I have to travel halfway around the world to find you and take care of you?" For a moment, Joe's heart stopped. The voice had a familiar Brooklyn, New York, twang to it. It sounded like Vinnie Niemann, a close classmate of his from Navigation School at Monroe, Louisiana. But it could not be! Vinnie had been reported MIA, (missing in action), about nine months ago. The last word Joe had on his close friend was that he was last seen parachuting earthward, having jumped from his crippled B-17 after a bomb run over Hamburg, Germany.

Joe jumped to his feet and turned to see the most beautiful sight. Vinnie Niemann was standing there, tall and thin, with a lip-stretching grin that ran from ear to ear. The two young American flyers, both lieutenants, were not ashamed to hug and cry as they fumbled for words to celebrate the occasion. They both tried to talk at the same time, neither one getting very far. Then Joe put up his hand and said, "Okay, Vinnie, you first." He took a pace backwards and studied his pal. Vinnie seemed skinnier and taller than he had been back in the States. Joe then took Vinnie back to his barracks where he introduced him to Nuffrie. The twosome immediately became a threesome. The chemistry was positive.

As the days dwindled down, the scarcity of food began to increase its toll on the Kriegies. They became thinner, more lethargic, and spent much of their time lying on their bunks. Even the local German population was feeling the pinch. It was becoming more difficult to barter with them for food.

On one particular occasion, Joe had to give four packages of Chesterfield cigarettes for one hen's egg, a small one at that. But, nevertheless, it was an egg, a sight Joe had not seen for nearly six months. He and Nuffrie had an unspoken pact about food. It was a "share and share alike" feeling. In fact, during the early days at Stalag VII-A, Nuffrie had become ill from some sort of stomach flu. He was quite nauseous and could not eat his allotted meals. He offered his food to Joe, who would have accepted the offer under normal conditions. But, as tempting as the offer was, Joe did not have the heart to accept it. Instead, he wrapped the food in wax paper retrieved from a small cereal box and saved it until Nuffrie was well enough to eat it himself.

And so, the division of the egg became a challenging problem. The cooking of the egg was not a problem. The cutting it into two equal bites was the difficulty. Other Kriegies within earshot of the discussion offered their unsolicited advice. One Kriegie suggested that the egg be soft boiled, pin pricked on both ends and sucked. High card would be picked to determine who sucked first, Joe or Nuffrie. They would be allowed to alternate by taking swallows until the egg shell was empty. Another bystander suggested that since the egg was so small, straws should be drawn and the winner eat the whole egg himself. Of course Joe and Nuffrie did not take any of this advice seriously, but it did draw a laugh from the small crowd that had gathered to witness the event. They were curious as to how the egg was to be cooked and divided evenly so that both Joe and Nuffrie would be satisfied that the process was absolutely fair.

Finally, after more discussion and suggestions, they decided to cook the egg, over easy. After it was cooked, one of them would cut the morsel into two equal pieces, and the other would choose which half he wanted. This method required that the ultimate in fairness be observed. Joe set up his small tin can stove, fueled it, lighted it, and fed it with his supply of illegal wood splinters. Then he applied a small amount of margarine on a flat tin, which he had fashioned from an empty soup can that came in a Red Cross food parcel. When the flat tin reached the right temperature, Joe carefully cracked the egg and poured it in the center of the hot tin. Everyone within visual range watched as the egg slowly gelled, forming a white border around a yellow center. Then with a homemade spatula, he carefully picked up the half-cooked egg and gingerly flipped it over. Good job. The yolk was still intact. Joe left the egg on the heated tin long enough so that the "over easy" was really "over hard." This made it easier to cut and eliminate oozing.

Now it was time to draw cards to see who would cut and who would choose. Nuffrie drew first and pulled a nine of diamonds. Not a bad card. Then Joe rolled up his sleeve in an exaggerated gesture, and pulled the jack of spades. So, Joe opted to choose rather than cut. Nuffrie, knife in hand, stood back in a melodramatic manner to eye the cooked egg. He carefully laid the knife on the center of the egg with an exaggerated motion and sliced it into two pieces. Joe thought he detected Nuffrie's hand tremble as he committed the deed.

Now it was Joe's turn to make a historic decision. He eyed the split egg from all angles. Then he stepped back and stroked his chin. He decided to take the right half of the egg. He picked it up with his fork, sprinkled a dash of salt on it, and in one gulp, chewed and swallowed it. The witnessing Kriegies broke out into spontaneous applause. That was the first egg that Joe had tasted since that fateful day of November 16, 1944, when ABLE ONE was shot down over the bomb run at Innsbruck, Austria.

It was early April. The morning broke with a crispness that reminded Joe of a New England spring. The sky was crystal clear. Not a cloud in sight. The rising sun had no trouble bathing the European countryside with its warm blanket of hope. Lovoi thought of home again. He wondered if his family ever got word that he was alive and well. What a miserable Thanksgiving and Christmas they must have had. His thoughts traveled halfway around the world to the Pacific Theater where his brothers, Ben and Sam, were seeing action against the Japanese armies. He prayed that they were well.

Then he thought of his married sister Anna, back home in Cambridge, Massachusetts. He remembered a story she told him about the time that she was coming to America with her mother, Nancy, and brothers, Ben and Sam, and sisters, Rosalie and Nerina. They were on a boat from Palermo, Italy, to New York where the man of the family, Ottavio, was waiting for them. He remembered this story because Anna's heroic act saved Ben's life and he prayed God to save it again. In the early days of ocean travel, the passage across the Atlantic took the better part of three weeks. It was a very expensive trip. The Lovois were traveling steerage class, i.e., in the ship's hold. The conditions were very unsanitary and unhealthy. If a passenger were to die during the early part of the trip, there was no way that the ship's authorities could preserve the corpse until the trip was over. So, it was a common practice to dispose of the body by delivering it into the sea. Joe had Ben on his mind, and perhaps that is why he thought of the incident.

Early on this trip to New York, Ben, just four years old, was struck with a serious form of influenza. The ship's doctor quarantined him in the hospital quarters, which were below deck. Neither Nancy, his mother, nor any of his siblings were allowed to visit him because of the possibility of spreading the infection. After several days of watching Nancy weep over her inability to visit Ben, Anna, then eight years old, took matters into her own hands. She quietly slipped away from her mother and made a bee line for the hospital quarters. As she entered, unnoticed, the quarantine section, she heard Ben crying.

Anna spotted him desperately trying to climb out of his crib. At the same time, Ben spotted Anna as she ran toward him. He screamed her name, but she put her finger up to her mouth in a gesture to be quiet. Then she picked him up, ran from the hospital area, avoiding the hospital authorities, and did not stop running until she deposited Ben in Nancy's lap. Nancy's joy was boundless as she embraced this frightened little boy. There was no way she would return him to the ship's authorities now. As luck would have it, several kind sailors were helpful in keeping Ben hidden until the incident blew over. They even were able to bring fresh food and milk to Nancy for Ben's feedings. The miracle of this story was that Anna, an eight-year-old, had the nerve to do what she did because she feared that Ben would be buried at sea. Now, Ben was in Guadalcanal in the South Pacific, fighting for his life again.

The warm spring weather was welcome at Stalag VII-A. Some of the healthier Kriegies were taking their walks without wearing their coats. April brought a pervasive air of optimism to the Stalag. The funny looking portable tin can stoves were everywhere. Since the fuel supply was getting scarcer, they were only used once a day to heat the evening meals. At dusk the reflections of these stoves gave an eerie ambiance to the prison compound. Lovoi thought it looked like a candlelight vigil in a greedy graveyard full of ghoulish shadows.

Mid-April was accompanied by unusually warm weather. Snow was melting fast, adding to the spring rainfall. The prison campgrounds were deep in mud. The latrine began to fill to capacity. The Germans had no fuel for the trucks (honey wagons) to be driven to the pump-out location of the latrine. The stench was unbearable. The Allied senior officer made strong demands on the camp Commander to clean up the situation before an epidemic broke out. The German commander explained his plight to the Allied senior officer. The Kriegies had no leverage in the argument. The unsanitary situation was a time bomb. In a matter of days, the latrine could not be used any further. Its contents were spilling over onto the walkways, making it impossible to use the facility without stepping on waste products.

The Allied senior officer decided that these drastic conditions demanded drastic actions. He had already protested the situation through the formal channels. He gave the German commandant more than enough time to correct the problem. So, now he used the only weapon he had left. He ordered his men not to show up at the next *appel.*

When the time came for the next *appel,* the guards found no one to be counted. The Kriegies remained indoors, ignoring the *appel.* The guards entered barrack after barrack and literally shoved and pushed the Kriegies outdoors. But just as fast as they were able to line up ten or twenty Kriegies in a straight line, they all dispersed while the guards went in search of more prisoners. And so it went for a while until the Goons realized that

"Appel"

their tactics would not result in an accurate count of the POW's. The guards disappeared.

Everyone wondered what next? It did not take long for them to stop wondering. The guards returned with a pack of German Shepherd attack dogs. The dogs were very efficient in moving the Kriegies into somewhat of a line. But, again, as soon as the guards left to get more Kriegies, those who were about to be counted dispersed in all directions. Again the guards left the scene and before any of the Kriegies could wonder what was next, they reappeared. This time they were not only leading leashed dogs in one hand, but they held loaded pistols in the other hand. The stakes had just been raised. No one wanted to die at this late stage of captivity with liberation not far away.

But again the Kriegies cautiously held out. There was no way that they were going to be still long enough to be counted. Was the German commandant bluffing? Was it worth even one man's life to find out? While Joe was pondering these questions, he felt the muzzle of one of the dogs press against his leg. He jumped back and pretended to line up for the *appel*. By now the whole compound was in an uproar. Things were quickly getting out of control. Then just as suddenly as this whole fiasco began, it ended. The armed guards were recalled by their superior. The German commandant and the senior Allied officer had further discussions.

Nearly an hour later, the Allied officer came out of the headquarters and ordered his men to "fall in" for *appel*. The Kriegies lined up quickly, were counted, and dismissed. They wondered if their senior officer had given in to the German demands. They did not have to wonder very long because before evening was upon them, the "honey wagons" rolled into the compound and cleaned

159

out the latrine. Lovoi sighed and believed he had dodged another bullet. The conversation that evening was concerning whether the German commandant was bluffing or not. But as one English playwright and poet said, "All's well that ends well."

From the clandestine radio reports the Kriegies were getting, the Allied offensive was picking up momentum. The German resistance was cracking along the Western front. Allied fighter aircraft were flying scouting missions looking for targets and destroying any resistance they met. On several occasions, the P-38 and P-51 American fighters flew over Stalag VII-A and wagged their wings in recognition.

One day in late April, a P-51 came out of nowhere and buzzed the camp at very low level. The Kriegies were unprepared for such a show. Some of them thought it was a German fighter at first. They ran into the barracks and ducked under the bottom bunks, expecting to be strafed. One young American lieutenant screamed hysterically and had to be restrained until it was over. Yes, nerves were raw, stress was high, and anticipation was rampant. During the last week of April, the Kriegies were ordered to stay indoors because the fighting was close enough for errant gun shots to be intercepted.

The Kriegies looked through cracks in the barracks walls and could see the Allied advance through the adjacent fields around the camp. The sound of gunfire and artillery grew louder with each passing day. The German guards were on the alert. It looked like they were prepared to die for the defense of the Stalag. The Kriegies were careful to stay inside where they would avoid being shot at by trigger-happy guards. Tension was building up throughout the prison. The end was near for the enemy, and for the Kriegies.

Finally, on the morning of May 7, 1945, the battle for Moosburg was over. Stalag VII-A assumed a deadly silence. The Kriegies peered out the dirty windows and could not see any of the guards. The watchtowers were empty. No one knew what to do. Was it a trick to get the Kriegies to break out where they could be killed? Slowly, the Kriegies opened the barracks doors and ventured out just a few feet. They strained to find any guard. As time elapsed, they got braver and braver. One of them even climbed up one of the watchtowers and verified that it was abandoned.

The Allied senior officer called the men to attention and told them to sit tight until further orders. He was desperately trying to reach the Allied command for news of what was going on and what they should do in the meantime. He was unable to reach anybody with his clandestine radio. Late that afternoon the Kriegies spied a line of tanks approaching the camp from a hill just on the horizon. They were not sure if the tanks were friendly or enemy. As they drew closer, some of the keener eyed Kriegies recognized the tanks as American Sherman tanks. The news spread like wildfire. The men screamed and yelled with emotional delight. They could hardly wait for the tank column to reach them.

Then they spotted a jeep racing ahead of the tank column. It carried an American flag. A tall soldier was standing in the passenger side. He was helmeted and stood very straight. When the jeep was within fifty yards of the open front gate, the Kriegies recognized the tall straight soldier. He was General George Patton. His jeep came to a stop just inside the Stalag barbed-wire fence. He was immediately surrounded by hundreds of thin, brave, grateful, and homesick young men. The senior Allied officer made his way to the jeep and stood before the General. He snapped a sharp salute.

The General stood tall and returned the salute with the comment, "It is we who salute you and all these brave men." Then the two men embraced. It was a silent moment. Then a Kriegie who had talked the jeep driver into giving him the American flag climbed up the camp's flag pole and replaced the Nazi flag with the Stars and Stripes. A thunderous cheer erupted that moment at Stalag VII-A, which could be heard as far west as New York City. It was a very moving sight to see thousands of young men looking up at the American flag as tears streamed unashamedly down their grimy youthful faces. The POW's climbed all over the Fourteenth Armored Division tanks as the liberating Army troops handed out C-Rations to the starving Kriegies.

Patton: a welcomed hero

Patton salutes the Kriegies

Liberation at Stalag VII A Moosburg

POW's patching up their clothes

X

Victory, A Medal, and Paris

General Patton stood back a few paces and ordered all Kriegies to stand "At Ease" for the duration of his visit. Then he was escorted on an inspection tour of the entire camp. He seemed to be more interested in the living conditions and the treatment accorded the Kriegies than he was in the actual hardships they endured. He was humorously impressed when he was shown the tin can stoves and how they worked. He tried to speak to as many Kriegies as possible. At one point he asked Lovoi a question regarding the Red Cross food parcels. Lovoi explained that the Germans kept at least half of them for their own use, and that they were almost as much in need of food as the Kriegies. He grunted an oath to show his disapproval of that practice.

Joe had a good look at the General. He stood next to him as he spoke to the senior Allied officer. The General was tall, all right. He looked like an American cowboy with his pearl six-shooters strapped to his sides. He exuded an air of confidence. Joe was thankful that he was on the Allied side of the war.

Within the hour an American two-and-one-half-ton truck sped into the compound. It carried about two dozen new aluminum trash barrels full of canned goods and five-gallon cans of water. As each barrel was unloaded, dozens of

Food, water, and Heaven

Kriegies reached their hands into them and pulled out cans of food. There was chicken, turkey, ham, beef stew, salmon, pasta, and meat loaf. When Joe was lucky enough to squeeze his hand through the crowd and into the barrel, he pulled out a can of spaghetti and meat balls. The Kriegies were warned not to stuff themselves because such a move would be unwise. It might cause stomach cramps due to the sudden impact of food intake to the digestive system.

The General visited with the liberated troops for the rest of the early evening. But later in the evening, he boarded his jeep and raced to catch up to his tank column. He did leave several of his armored vehicles at the Stalag as protection for the Kriegies in case of any sporadic flare-ups. A temporary War Crimes Investigating Team set up operations and began interrogating some of the Kriegies. It took three more days to complete the plans to evacuate the thousands of Kriegies. They were to be trucked to several small airports surrounding the Munich area, and from there they were to be airlifted to a rehabilitation camp in France. It was going to be a long, drawn-out process to administer the paperwork that had to be completed before the healing phase could be started.

During the three-day wait, some of the POW's took short trips into Moosburg and visited with the civilians. They brought back souvenirs and stories. The natives were friendly and warm toward the Kriegies. A few of the POW's went to see the death camp at Dachau. When they returned to the stalag, they described the horrors and shocking scenes they had witnessed. The slaughter and suffering that the inmates of this death camp went through was the lowest form of man's inhumanity to man. Several of the Kriegies were sick when they got back to camp from that unbelievable experience.

Liberation: the day it ended

The penalties of savage dehumanization

The war was over. Hitler had committed suicide. The Russians had taken Berlin. Chaos was prevalent throughout the European Theater of Europeans. Joe, Nuffrie, and Vinnie stayed close to camp, having come this far all in one piece. Some of the more adventurous Kriegies went visiting the border towns. Joe and his companions were eventually trucked to the Augsburg airport, about an hour drive from Stalag VII-A. They had to wait until the next day before the troop carrier C-47's arrived to start the evacuation process. It felt a little odd for these Kriegies, ex-airmen, to be flying again in a military aircraft. The absence of flak was very noticeable, and everyone had something to say about that. The flight to the rehabilitation center was without incident and took about two hours.

When they landed, the Kriegies were informed that the camp was called Camp Lucky Strike. This camp was to be their home for the time that it took to prepare transportation back to the States. In the interim they were to get all kinds of shots, a thorough physical examination, nourishing food, psychiatric treatment, and lots of rest. The Kriegies were looking forward to all of the above, except lots of rest. They were too excited to be still. They were looking for lost comrades as well as trying to get word to their parents that they were well and on their way home.

Camp Lucky Strike was a very large operation. It had complete facilities, which included clinics, hospital rooms, exercise rooms, mess halls, recreation dens, movies, and lecture halls. Kriegies were here from all over Europe, having been liberated from all types of prison camps. There was lots to do at Camp Lucky Strike, but definitely the most favorite activity was eating. Warnings about eating habits were issued on a daily basis. The

172

results of overeating did take their toll on some of the POW's who got very sick. It was rumored that a few of them died. Following the physical examinations, the Kriegies were put on the appropriate medications that would begin to heal their bodies. Camp Lucky Strike was a reunion mecca for long lost buddies and separated comrades. If all the war stories that were told there were to be written and bound, the result would be volumes of exciting reading for a lifetime.

The most frequent complaints of the POW's were dysentery, skin disorders, and gastrointestinal ailments. These complaints were treated on the spot. The psychological problems were more complex. These problems were initially treated at the camp, but their healing would take much longer. These problems had to be treated back in the States where facilities and trained manpower were available. The more seriously sick Kriegies were airlifted to various medical centers in the U.S.

The rest of them were to travel by boat to the United States. However, some of those POW's scheduled to sail for the States did not want to go home right away. They wanted to spend some time in Europe first. The commanding officers at Camp Lucky Strike forbade any of the Kriegies from traveling without a pass. And there were no passes to be had. It was difficult enough to herd thousands of POW's within the confines of a camp. It would be almost impossible to keep track of them if they were allowed to cruise the various European countries.

But, when Lovoi, Niemann, and Brancato discussed the possibility of prolonging their stay, it ended in three decisions. Vinnie wanted to visit Paris, Joe had no opinion and said he would do what the majority wanted to do, and Nuffrie wanted to go back home to Ohio on the first boat that would take him. Vinnie argued that they were just a few hundred miles from Paris and only God knew if and when they would have another opportunity to see Paris, the "City of Lights." Vinnie convinced Joe that it was a good idea, but Nuffrie held fast to his desire to go home. And so it was decided that Joe and Vinnie would see Nuffrie off on the first boat that would take him, and they would figure out how to skip camp and get to Paris.

Some of the Kriegies had already skipped out and ended up in the Baltic countries and Sweden, visiting relatives. They were eventually rounded up and returned to Camp Lucky Strike. During the next few days, Nuffrie scanned the posted rosters for his name to find out when he was to leave. In the meantime, of course, the Kriegies were issued all new clothing from inside out. It was very luxurious to feel the clean cotton.

Additionally, they were issued a portion of their back pay. So now they not only had new clothing, but money in their pockets as well. Then they were issued a complete set of toiletries and given a trip to the barber shop. The physical changes that were taking place in their appearances were indeed astonishing. Most of the young men could not hide their weight loss and gaunt expressions, but after even one week of nourishment and rest, they were beginning to fill out and look better.

It was now getting to the end of May, 1945. The war in Europe was won. Only pockets of minor resistance remained to be mopped up. The Allied emphasis was now focused on the Pacific war. The Allies were making plans to finish off the Japanese and try to get the peace process started. Most of Europe was celebrating the war's end. And Paris was no exception.

Two days later the roster of Kriegies who were scheduled to depart for the States was posted. Lovoi, Brancato, kand Niemann were named to be ready to be trucked to the port of Le Havre by 8:00 A.M. next morning. Lovoi and Niemann said their good-byes to Brancato, and somehow, they were not on the truck to Le Havre the next morning. They must have overslept. Now that they had missed their boat ride, Joe and Vinnie were more determined than ever to visit Paris. The long cold months of captivity had taken their toll. Their young, brutalized minds and bodies seemed to be reaching out for some kind of payback. And that payback was a trip to Paris.

Like all the other Kriegies, Lovoi went through the repatriation cycle during which he was pleasantly surprised. He was notified that he had been promoted to First Lieutenant as of November 9, 1944, and also that he had been awarded the Distinguished Flying Cross (DFC) for bravery over and above the call of duty. He was not flying through "Cloud Nine," he was sitting on it.

Vinnie and Joe decided that the sooner they "escaped" from Camp Lucky Strike for Paris, the better. That evening during their supper at one of the long tables in the mess hall, they were putting the finishing touches on their "escape" plans. While they were discussing the details of the plan, a group of military "brass" entered the mess hall. To their pleasant surprise, the group of VIP's was led by none other than General Dwight D. Eisenhower, the Supreme Commander of all forces in the European Theater of Operations. Joe and Vinnie jumped to their feet and snapped a smart salute. The general returned the salute and with his characteristic grin, waved them "At Ease."

On the next morning, "Tom Sawyer and Huckleberry Finn" packed their musette bags and casually walked toward the rear of the camp. There was little or no activity there and their chances of not being noticed were much better in this remote area. The first phase of the "escape plan" was to jump over the perimeter fence and disappear into the wooded area that abutted the camp. They succeeded in jumping the fence and disappearing into the wooded area. They ran hard for about two or three hundred yards. Then they lay down and listened. For almost a minute, neither of them spoke while they caught their breath. They heard no alarms or whistles, so they decided to go on with their plan.

They walked a wide semi-circle, concentric with the camp's perimeter. When they calculated that they had walked far enough, they made a right turn and looked for the main road that led into the camp entrance. Sure enough they found it and they were well out of sight of the Military Police who were manning the front gate. They stepped to the side of the road leading east toward Paris and waited for a lift.

Several minutes later a delivery truck rounded the curve and slowed down. When the driver noticed that these two well-dressed, young American officers had their thumbs up and were pointing in the direction of Paris, he stopped and offered them a lift. When the driver of the truck, an English-speaking Frenchman, was told that the two hitchhikers were on their way to Paris, he apologetically stated that he was not going as far as Paris, but he would be happy to let them off in the city of Rouen. He pointed out to Joe and Vinnie that Rouen was on the way to Paris and that they should be successful in being picked up at the outskirts of Rouen.

Since the Kriegies had no hard and fast arrival schedule to Paris, they adopted a "devil may care" attitude and decided to enjoy every minute of their stolen freedom. The sun was shining, the sky was blue, and the morning rain had washed the countryside clean. The two young friends were happy and it showed. They were joking and laughing. It was great to be alive. The driver sensed the reason for their enthusiasm and suggested that as long as they were in the vicinity of Rouen, they might enjoy visiting some of the ancient structures there.

As the morning blended into the noon hour, the road traffic grew heavier. If they passed a military vehicle, or were passed by one, both Joe and Vinnie ducked under the dashboard of the truck so they could not be seen. The smiling driver caught on to the situation and nodded his approval. They arrived safely and without being detected in Rouen about noontime. The driver let them off in front of a *patisserie,* a French bakery. They stopped just long enough to eat a sweet roll and wash it down with a cup of café.

It was early afternoon when they took up their thumbing positions on the road east to Paris. It was not long before an American jeep, driven by an Army major stopped and offered them a ride. When he learned that the two adventurers were on their way to Paris, he stated that he was heading for a city called Rheims, which was located about a hundred miles northeast of Paris. He suggested that they spend a short time visiting the Cathedral of Notre Dame there before hitchhiking to Paris. He promised that it would be well worth the time.

They accepted the lift gratefully and off they went to Rheims. The major was kind enough to drop them off right in front of the cathedral. The young men had to crane their necks as far back as they could in order to see the very top of the cathedral. It was an awesome sight. It towered high above the adjacent buildings. It had taken nearly two hundred years to build this church. It is the most perfect example of Gothic architecture in France. Joe had never seen a church this large in his entire life. Vinnie had seen St. Patrick's Cathedral in Manhattan and said the two churches compared in size and architecture.

Since the two Kriegies wanted to be in Paris by dinner time, they did not spend any more time in Rheims. They headed for the road to Paris and raised their thumbs again. Within minutes of assuming their position, an American jeep bearing two MP's (Military Police) came into view. The jeep stopped abreast of Vinnie and Joe. The MP in the passenger side politely asked to see their identification papers and their leave authorizations. When the two young officers could not provide the MP's with satisfactory leave papers, they requested that Vinnie and Joe get into the back seat of the jeep. They were driven to a small army outpost at the edge of the city of Rheims. They were escorted to a wooden holding cell with a barbed-wire window and a door with a padlock. They were told that they would be returned to Camp Lucky Strike on the next MP vehicle that was going in that direction. The MP's were very sympathetic to their story about being liberated POW's and that they just wanted to see Paris before they went home. But the MP's were unwilling to close their eyes to their lack of passes.

Vinnie and Joe sat on a bench inside the holding cell and cursed their luck. Joe tried to ease the tension by stating that the trip was worth the risk since they had already seen Rouen and Rheims. But Vinnie was not quite ready to accept this unexpected fate. He examined the room and noticed that the barbed wire crossing the window was stapled to the framework of the window. He pulled out a nail file and began to work loose the heavy staples that held the barbed wire in place. He commented that they came out rather easily. Joe pulled out a nail clipper from his pocket and joined Vinnie in removing the barbed wire.

Between the efforts of the two of them, they removed enough of the wire so they could open the window and squeeze their thin bodies through it. They worked quickly because they did not know how much time they had. Joe was thankful that he had Vinnie as an accomplice, because only a Brooklynite would have the nerve and the cleverness to dare an escape. The more thought that Joe gave to the unfairness of what was happening to him and Vinnie, the more determined he became to escape to Paris and enjoy the payback.

It took a matter of minutes to remove the barbed wire from the window frame. The window was easily opened. The two Kriegies squeezed through the opening one at a time, and ran like hell as fast and as far as they could through the wooded area behind the holding cell. They did not stop until they had no more breath, then for only as long as it took to fill their lungs again. Then they ran some more as if their very lives depended upon it. Finally, they stopped to get their bearings. They made sure that their route was away from Rheims. They were not sure that they would find a way out, but they had no choice. They just kept on walking in the hope that they would find a road that would direct them out of the woods.

After a short while, they came upon a dirt road that showed recent passage of horse-drawn vehicles. Since this was their only option, they decided to walk down this road and hope for the best. They walked in silence for nearly half an hour. Then Vinnie put his hand up to his ear and turned his head. "Did you hear that?" he asked Joe. They both stopped and listened. "Yes, I hear it!" Joe responded. "It sounds like a lawn mower."

They ran off the road and into the abutting wooded area and waited for whatever it was to show itself. They breathed a sigh of relief when they identified the vehicle as a large open wagon, powered by a noisy engine, and driven by a man who was smoking a pipe. He was wearing a wide-brim straw hat and a light jacket. The two American hitchhikers strolled out of the woods and waved for the truck to stop. The surprised Frenchman slowed to a stop and poked his head out the driver's window. Lovoi tried to explain that the two American soldiers needed a lift to Paris.

At first the Frenchman did not understand what Lovoi was trying to say. But when he heard the word "Paris," his eyes lit up and he nodded vigorously. He offered them a seat beside him and off they went. From the looks of the produce piled into the wagon, it appeared that the driver was a truck farmer who was on his way to Paris to deliver the day's pickings to the many eateries in that city. The driver reached back into a small basket, pulled out two large red apples, and offered one to each of the hitchhikers. Vinnie and Joe graciously accepted them. They wiped them on their sleeves and enjoyed their flavor.

It was nearly three hours later when the truck pulled into the outskirts of Paris. Lovoi felt the excitement beginning to awake within him. What a wonderful moment! Paris in the spring! It seemed like a fitting climax to his overseas adventure, including the flight over the Atlantic, the stationing in Foggia, the twenty-nine bombing missions, the POW nightmare, and the emotional wrench of liberation.

The evening was well under way. It was past nine o'clock. The city was crowded. The driver drove out of his way to deposit the two young American officers within a short walk of the Arc de Triomphe. He used sign language to assure them that they could easily walk to most of the tourist attractions, restaurants, and hotels. Then he shook their hands and wished them good luck. From their vantage point at the base of the Arc de Triomphe, they could make out the silhouette of the Eiffel Tower against the nearly dark horizon. In another direction they could see the famous lighted wide avenue known as Champs Elysées. It was very alive, with happy pedestrians traveling its sidewalks in both directions.

The war was over and Parisians were still celebrating that event even two weeks later. There were young people, middle-aged people, and senior citizens mixing together. They all seemed to be happy and excited. As Joe and Vinnie elbowed their way through the crowds, they were greeted with smiles and friendly waves. The young Americans had no definite plans for the evening. They did wish to dine at some point but not alone. They were hoping to meet two young ladies with whom they could exchange small talk and companionship. They were not sure of whom they were looking for, but they were sure they would recognize the moment.

They took two seats at a table in an outdoor café and ordered two beers. As they sat and enjoyed the refreshing taste of the mild beverage, they watched the promenading humanity. They tried to make eye contact with some of the younger ladies who were walking by. By the time they had finished drinking their beer, the quest was over. Two young, well-dressed ladies, a tall slim brunette and a shorter, more shapely redhead, glanced in their direction and smiled. The surprised young Americans rose to their feet as a team and invited the ladies to join them at their table for libation and conversation. The ladies seemed pleased to accept the invitation, and then the fun began—overcoming the language barrier.

Joe's limited knowledge of Italian did not help much. Vinnie's more limited knowledge of German helped even less. And the ladies limited knowledge of the English language was almost as useless. But, the backlash of this language barrier was a pleasant atmosphere created by four friendly young people trying to be even more friendly. What little effective language was accomplished needed a rather animated behavior to be understood.

The last time Joe and Vinnie were seen together in Paris, they were strolling down the Champs Elysées, arm in arm and four abreast, with two beautiful Parisian ladies. They were headed for a small intimate café to share a memorable dinner. They stopped just long enough to purchase two small bouquets of spring flowers for their two new friends. As they approached the café, Joe sneaked a side glance at his redheaded date, and he was rewarded with the most beautiful smile since Lucia.

They entered the small intimate café where the maitre d' graciously sat the foursome at a private table. While they were trying to translate the menu, Joe looked up at his date for help. At that moment he thought he caught the two ladies wink at each other as they ordered from the wine list. He might have been mistaken, but then again he might not.

Happy ending—Paris in the Spring

Epilogue

Obviously Lieutenant Lovoi survived World War II in spite of the ever-present and haunting specter of death each time he climbed aboard a B-17. The year 1995 measured the fiftieth anniversary of the end of the war, as well as his discharge from the military service. For all those fifty years, he spoke very little of the experiences you have just read about in *LISTEN . . . My Children.*

During those years, whenever his thoughts wandered back to those days, he somehow was able to find an excuse or a reason to push those memories back into his subconscious mind and tag them with a label "Not Yet." Oddly enough, he did begin to write this true story just months after his discharge. He struggled with the first two chapters until he tried to describe the bomb run over the Innsbruck railroad yards. Then suddenly, the motivation and the energy to continue the narrative unexplainably left him. His young life became preoccupied with returning to civilian life and getting a good education under his belt.

This academic achievement was uninterruptedly followed by a successful career as an electrical engineer and physicist. After about a dozen years of designing and developing electronic systems at RCA, he decided to start his own manufacturing company. His company survived the next twenty-four years, during which he was the CEO. In the interim, he had sired five wonderful children.

He also joined the Air Force Reserve, in which he holds the rank of Captain. This story had to wait. His brothers Sam and Sal lived through the war unscathed. His brother Ben was wounded in the Guadalcanal Campaign.

Then, just as suddenly as the urge to stop writing this story hit him in 1945, the opposite urge possessed him in 1995. He needed to write this story. He got out of bed one morning, recovered his dusty fifty-year-old manuscript, slipped a sheet of paper in his IBM typewriter, and began pulling at his memory. Slowly, and sometimes painfully, he was able to piece together the chronological episodes that eventually were published. He was somewhat surprised that the memories he was recalling in 1995 were just as vivid as they were when they occurred in 1944–1945. He wryly marveled that he could remember scenes that happened fifty years ago, yet he had some difficulty when it came time to remember his last week's appointments. He is convinced that man has a selective memory and a convenient one at that.

There were times when the speed of the typewriter could not keep up with the outpouring of data from the past. There were times when the typewriter was unusually quiet as the author groped for just the right word or phrase to describe a moment that required absolute accuracy. And there were also times when he had difficulty in reading what was being typed because his view was clouded by his tears. He felt as though he had to complete an unfinished painting. The only way to do it was to live it again—a painful decision.

It was late in the spring of 1995 that he joined the ranks of an ex-POW group that met weekly in the Veterans Administration Boston Outpatient Clinic. The moderator of this weekly forum is Bob Daniels, a very qualified employee of the Veterans Administration. His compassion and encouragement for the aging ex-POW's have kept them together where the successful results of group therapy are quite evident. Only an ex-POW can understand and feel the survival instinct that was lived through by these men. They are all very different, but they share one common denominator: cheating death, the hard way!

Some of the ex-POW's are still angry at the enemy. Some have forgiven him. Some feel that our government has forgotten them. Some feel grateful for the benefits they receive. Some are secretly ashamed to admit that they are ex-POWs because it smacks of the act of surrender. Some realize that they had no choice and are lucky to be alive. Some of them have friends who are critical of their misfortune, while others have friends who admire their courage. Most of them still carry around the physical scars of their capture and captivity, while a few of them were lucky to have avoided any wounds. But all of them, without exception, are still plagued by the mental torture caused by nightmares, anxiety, depression, and survivor guilt.

It was here at this clinic that Lovoi met a Veterans Administration doctor, a psychiatrist. Her name is Victoria Russell. Dr. Russell has devoted much of her young life to the care and mending of the warped and broken lives of ex-POW's. She helped Joe understand why it took so long, fifty years, for him to share his military experiences, and why he sobbed uncontrollably when she gently prodded his memory to release the details of those experiences. She pieced together his past survivor guilt with his present difficulty in handling it. She encouraged him to write this book and distribute it to the generations that follow. She explained that it was part of the therapeutic program that he would require toward the normalization of the rest of his life.

Without frequent reminders of man's inhumanity to man, the lessons taught by the Bataan Death March, the Holocaust, the Rape of Nanking, the atomic obliteration of two large Japanese industrial centers, and the ashes in London, Tokyo, and Berlin, would soon be forgotten. This planet's progeny must learn about these atrocities and be determined never to allow them to happen again.

Dr. Russell pointed out that Joe had been able to contain the psychological effects of his war for such a long time because his "workaholic" lifestyle was able to suppress and overshadow them. But in his later years, the psychological damage caused by the POW experience could no longer be contained. And it was in Dr. Russell's office that the gist of the story that you have just read, was told for the first time by Lovoi. Dr. Russell helped him to readjust more of his black-and-white world into the color gray.

In May, 1995, nearly the whole world took note of the fiftieth anniversary of the end of World War II, know as VE Day. During this occasion, Joe and his son, Joseph, were in London, England, on an educational tour. It was here, during the celebration of VE Day, that he began to feel the pangs of anxiety and depression to the extent that he had never felt them before. At first he thought that he felt this way because he was so close to the scene that had caused his trauma in the first place. But when the pangs continued to haunt him as the celebration went on, he realized that the condition was real and permanent. The British news and television reports were reliving the last days of the war. They underscored the total victory aspect of the "Unconditional Surrender" ultimatum. Even the Queen Mother was seen at every function as she thanked the brave veterans who came to London from all parts of the world to participate in this hallowed celebration. She plucked the emotional chords of many in the audiences when she asked for moments of silence so individuals could honor the brave and courageous warriors who had made the supreme sacrifice and were buried on European soil.

The skies were full of low-flying vintage war planes during the week of the celebration. There were American planes, like B-17, B-24, P-51, P-38, and P-40. There were the notable British planes, like the Spitfires, Hurricanes, Lancasters, and DeHavilands. Joe felt emotional conflict as these scenes played before his eyes. They brought back memories that had been buried for a long time. He tried not to show the sad effects when his son Joseph was facing him. He shielded his eyes from the sun as he studied the waves of bombers and fighters flying not very high above the rooftops. He did not understand why he had difficulty in controlling himself. At times he could not stop the tears as hard as he tried to.

The feelings of anxiety and depression continued to plague him throughout the weeks that followed the London experience. The United States was also in the midst of celebrating VE Day. Since Washington D.C. was the place to be for this, and since Joe had promised his son a visit to the nation's capital for his birthday, they both went to Washington for a long weekend.

Joe, Jr. was delighted to visit the Capitol. It had been a dream of his to see the historical sights that made America great. Like most young people, he enjoyed every minute of his visit. And Joseph, Sr. catered to his wishes to visit everything possible within the few days they had. They visited the Capitol Building, including both the

Senate and House chambers, the Washington Monument, the Smithsonian Institute, the White House, the Jefferson Memorial, and the Lincoln Memorial. It was during the long walk from the Capitol Building along the Mall that led to the Lincoln Memorial that Joseph felt an attack of depression. He did not know why, but he was sure that it had something to do with the Vietnam War Memorial, "The Wall." He avoided looking directly at "The Wall." He really did not want to see it. He hoped that his son would not ask to visit it on the way back from the Lincoln Memorial.

Well, Joseph, Jr. did notice "The Wall" and asked his father if they could visit it. His father hesitated, but Joseph promised to just take a quick look. Joseph, Sr. agreed and the two visitors strode toward the beginning of "The Wall," the low section. As they approached the low section of "The Wall," Joe, Jr. suggested that they try to read some of the names inscribed on the black marble. They did read a few of the names on that section. Joe, Sr. silently prayed for those brave young men whose lives had been snuffed out before they hardly began. He felt the shivers run down the back of his neck as they moved on to the next section of "The Wall." He could feel the tears welling under his eyelids as he tried to read more names. He could not see the names through the tears that he could not hold back. He turned his back to his son and wiped the wetness on his shirt sleeve. He tried to regain his composure before his son could see his difficulty. He was upset with himself for behaving in such an uncontrollable manner in front of his son. Wasn't he supposed to be a hard-nosed veteran?

Then, mercifully, he felt a young arm hug his shoulder and squeeze his bicep. And then, a tender voice said softly, "It's okay, Dad. We can go home now."

A Final Thought

John McCrae was a Canadian physician, soldier, and poet. And as the chief medical officer at a hospital in Boulogne, France, in World War I, he witnessed the suffering and death he wrote about. His most famous work from these writings is a poem he called, "In Flanders Fields."

In Flanders Fields

In Flanders fields the poppies blow
Between the crosses, row on row
That mark our place; and in the sky
The larks, still bravely singing, fly
Scarce heard amid the guns below.

We are the Dead. Short days ago
We lived, felt dawn, saw sunset glow,
Loved, and were loved, and now we lie
  In Flanders fields.

Take up our quarrel with this foe.
To you from failing hands we throw
"The torch"; be yours to hold it high.
If ye break faith with us who die
We shall not sleep, though poppies grow
  In Flanders fields.
    —John McCrae
    Dec. 8, 1915

(Reprinted courtesy of the National Archives of Canada—C26561.)

If you visit the cemetery at Flanders Fields and see the endless rows of neat white crosses, and if you *LISTEN* . . . *My Children* with undivided attention, you may be able to still hear a youthful chorus plead . . .

"We are the dead. Short days ago we lived, felt dawn, and saw sunset's glow. To you we throw the Torch!"

And as these words find their way into our grateful hearts we will realize that . . .

"We are the living. We feel dawn and see sunset glow. With outstretched arms we catch the Torch. *God help us if we drop it!*"